Tag, You're Knit!

Tag, You're Knit!

COLORFUL KNITS FOR KIDS

Mary Bonnette
Jo Lynne Murchland

LARK BOOKS

A Division of Sterling Publishing, Co., Inc.
New York / London

Senior Editor:
Valerie Van Arsdale Shrader

Editor:
Linda Kopp

Art Director:
Stacey Budge

Technical Editor:
Kay J. Hay

Illustrator:
Orrin Lundgren

Photographer:
Keith Wright

Cover Designer:
Cindy LaBreacht

Library of Congress Cataloging-in-Publication Data

Bonnette, Mary H., 1957-
  Tag, You're Knit! : colorful knits for kids / Mary Bonnette and Jo Lynne
Murchland. -- 1st ed.
      p. cm.
  Includes index.
  ISBN-13: 978-1-60059-159-4 (pb-trade pbk. : alk. paper)
  ISBN-10: 1-60059-159-0 (pb-trade pbk. : alk. paper)
  1. Knitting--Patterns. 2. Children's clothing. I. Murchland, Jo Lynne,
1938- II. Title.
  TT825.B649 2008
  746.43'2041--dc22
                                    2008004716

10 9 8 7 6 5 4 3 2 1

First Edition

Published by Lark Books, A Division of
Sterling Publishing Co., Inc.
387 Park Avenue South, New York, NY 10016

Text © 2008, Mary Bonnette and Jo Lynne Murchland
Photography © 2008, Lark Books unless otherwise specified
Illustrations © 2008, Lark Books unless otherwise specified

Distributed in Canada by Sterling Publishing,
c/o Canadian Manda Group, 165 Dufferina Street
Toronto, Ontario, Canada M6K 3H6

Distributed in the United Kingdom by GMC Distribution Services,
Castle Place, 166 High Street, Lewes, East Sussex, England BN7 1XU

Distributed in Australia by Capricorn Link (Australia) Pty Ltd.,
P.O. Box 704, Windsor, NSW 2756 Australia

If you have questions or comments about this book, please contact:
Lark Books
67 Broadway
Asheville, NC 28801
828-253-0467

Manufactured in China

ISBN 13: 978-1-60059-159-4

For information about custom editions, special sales, premium and corporate purchases,
please contact Sterling Special Sales Department at 800-805-5489 or specialsales@
sterlingpub.com.

Contents

Introduction..6

Getting Started 8

THE PROJECTS   **23**

Rib-It Mittens..24

Rib-It Hat 27

Leo the Lion 30

Sleepover Slippers 33

Loot Bags 36

Cable Guy Socks 39

Cable Guy Scarf..44

Leader of the Pack Sack 47

Button Belt 50

Perfect Pillows..52

Go Team..56

Listen Up! MP3 (or Cell) Case....................58

Funky Fanny Pack 60

EZ Leg Warmers 63

Pick Pocket for Boys 66

Pick Pocket for Girls 69

Strings & Stripes Scarf...............................72

Strings & Stripes Socks 74

Pink Parfait Scarf..78

Pink Parfait Hat 80

Derby Duds 82

Bella Bolero 85

Button Bag 90

Little Black Bag..92

Vested..94

Beautiful Belt 98

Knitting Techniques and Patterns 100

About the Authors......................................109

Acknowledgments 110

Index...111

Introduction

Designing for *Tag, You're Knit!* has been an absolutely delightful experience. For the past 12 years, we have been creating children's knitwear for catalogs, magazines, yarn companies, and our own line of patterns and kits. We also have authored several children's pattern books. As the owners of The Sassy Skein, our focus is children and their unique fit and style, but we've enjoyed this chance to branch out beyond traditional garments to fabulous and fashionable accessories.

In today's fashion world, accessories are IT. Children love color, they love funky, and they love to accessorize with flair. With 26 projects ranging from hats to socks, and from play to party, we have designs made to adorn from head to toe. Know a gadget fanatic? The Listen Up! MP3 (or Cell) Case (page 58) is sure to please. EZ Legwarmers (page 63) make a stand out accent for your little leading lady, while Sleepover Slippers (page 33) will keep youngsters' feet toasty. For that stylish someone with the independent spirit, knit up a sassy Button Belt (page 50) and Button Bag (page 90) set. And since children love to accessorize their rooms almost as much as themselves, we included a few home decor projects for wee ones like Perfect Pillows (page 52) and Leo the Lion (page 30).

Accessories are the perfect projects for beginner and experienced knitters alike; you can create any one of these marvelous projects with only a small amount of yarn and a short amount of time. If you're new to knitting, we hope this book serves as a colorful introduction to the wonderful world of hand knits. The Getting Started section covers all the supplies you'll need for your knitting tool bag as well as a host of color and design options perfect for infusing your projects with life. Next, you'll find an array of easy projects for the novice knitter in addition to some more advanced projects for the knitter with a few projects under his or her belt. If you need a refresher on techniques or stitch patterns, simply refer to the knitting techniques section at the back of the book (page 100).

As a creative fiber arts medium, knitting allows for a truly unique blend of vision and creativity with texture, color, shape, and function. We find that designing for children offers the freedom to combine these elements with all of the wonderful passion—and life and energy—of a child.

Getting Started

Let's face it: in today's fashion, it's all about the accessories. Never has this fashion theme been more wildly popular than with the youngest among us. Children from tots to tweens want to add pizzazz to their wardrobe with the latest and coolest "must have" accessories. This young, energetic generation thrives on the little goodies that make them feel unique and special. Easy, inexpensive, and ultra stylish, knitted accessories make for perfect children's gifts.

Children develop their own sense of style and taste at a very early age, so it helps to involve them, if possible, in the selection process before you undertake a knitting project. While you may want to knit a sensible scarf, they may prefer a backpack or colorful legwarmers. You may be in love with the yummy blue yarn in the yarn shop, and they may only have eyes for lime. What to do? Keep in mind that you want your intended recipient to feel special… and appreciate your labor of love. The great news is that there are endless color and design choices available; it's easy to make the selection process a win-win for everyone.

There are many designs in this book that you will need to knit to specific measurements. Whether it's the circumference of a head or the tiptoe of a foot, size will matter. To ensure a happy outcome, work with current measurements. Remember that children grow quickly, so measurements from six months ago are probably not very reliable. Take into consideration the child's probable growth rate for the time frame that it will take you to complete your project.

Whatever you create, make it bright and colorful. All kids, from tots to tweens, love colorful accessories.

Yarn

You finally have the perfect reason to knit that adorable children's project you've always pictured yourself making. You've picked out the pattern and decided on a color scheme, and you can already imagine the hours you'll spend knitting each loving stitch. But now, with so many options out there, you find yourself wondering how to go about choosing, and using, the correct yarn.

SELECTING YARNS FOR CHILDREN'S PROJECTS

We've put together a couple of key points to help you through the yarn selection process. First, consider the function of the project. Is laundering important? Dry cleaning is expensive and not practical for most children's garments, so be sure to choose a fiber that can withstand laundering. Many yarns can be hand washed carefully in cold water or laundered in your washer's delicate cycle and laid out flat to dry. Whereas your choices for washable yarns used to be limited to acrylics and other less-than-savory options, you now have a wide variety of beautiful and washable blends, cottons, and superwash wools to choose from.

All yarn labels clearly indicate the laundering care that should be given to the yarn. Pay close attention to this information. If you're knitting the project as a gift, consider tucking a yarn label in with the finished item to help the receiver understand how to care for their hand-knit gift.

When choosing a yarn for a child's project, keep in mind that it will likely lie next to soft, sensitive skin. Consider the fiber content in regard to how comfortable it will be for a child. It would be disappointing to have spent hours hand knitting something for your favorite little one, only to have them refuse to wear it because it's itchy.

The pattern or design of your intended project may require a specific type of yarn to give it a certain look. For example, if you're creating a sweater with an intarsia design (page 15), you may not want to use variegated yarns since they tend to minimize the clean lines you get with this type of design work. If you are felting a project, you'll need to use a wool yarn as opposed to a washable yarn, or your project won't felt properly. This guideline also applies to the texture of the yarn you choose. Ask yourself if a textured yarn is appropriate for your project before making your final selection.

While your little angel may only deserve the finest, consider the price of the yarn. Is the yarn that you want to use worth the price of the project? If not, look at similar yarns that might be less costly. Remember that children grow fast, and their use of an item may be short-lived due to a growth spurt. Keeping cost in mind, we do recommend that you use high-quality yarn. Your time and effort are valuable, and you don't want to waste them using a poor-quality yarn. But high quality doesn't necessarily mean expensive.

Finally, look to your pattern for suggested yarns. Knitting patterns should tell you what the model garment was knit out of, and this information will help steer you in the right direction. However, if you're adapting a pattern or not using one at all, you may have to substitute yarn. Next, we'll give you some tips on making smart yarn substitutions.

MAKING YARN SUBSTITUTIONS

Yarn substitution can be done easily if you pay attention to these three factors: the type of fiber called for in the pattern, the stitch gauge, and the total yardage required for your project. Consider these questions and guidelines to help decide what type of yarn to substitute.

Fiber Type

Should you use a natural yarn or a synthetic? Will you need to wash it by hand or washing machine? Should the yarn be a bulky weight or a thinner weight? Will it be worn next to the skin?

Stitch Gauge

What is the pattern's stitch gauge? Can you meet the gauge with the yarn you're considering? Do you knit tighter or looser than the average knitter? Can you control your gauge by moving up or down a needle size? Keep in mind that it's almost impossible to substitute a different weight of yarn and get the same results. For example, if your pattern calls for a DK weight, you'll have difficulty substituting a bulky weight yarn.

Total Yardage

Knitting patterns should always give you the total yardage needed for the project. To determine how many skeins you'll need to substitute, take the total yardage and divide it by the yardage of each skein you have chosen. For example, if the total needed is 550 yards (495 m) and you have 105-yard (95 m) skeins, divide 550 by 105. By this math, you'll need 5.25 skeins, or 6 skeins, to complete the project.

TIP

Leftover yarn? Save it! Everyone needs a stash. Scrap yarn can be used for future repairs, or to lengthen an item your little one is outgrowing. Or better yet, use your leftovers to teach a child to knit.

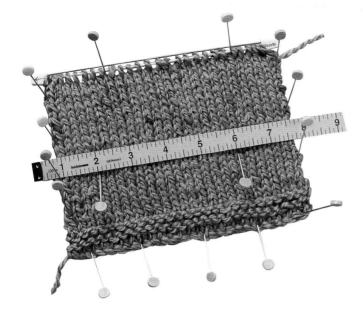

MAKING A GAUGE SWATCH

Whether you're using the yarn specified in your pattern or making a substitution, it's still very important to make a sample swatch before you begin your project. The swatch tells you how many stitches and how many rows you're getting per inch as you knit. Each of us has a slightly different knitting style. Until you work the sample swatch, you don't know if you'll get the same measurements for stitches and rows as outlined in the pattern.

A swatch should be worked as a 4-inch (10.2 cm) square in the pattern stitch you'll be knitting. Somewhere toward the center of your swatch, take the measurement for 1 inch (2.5 cm) of your work, and compare it with the specified stitch and row information given in your instructions. Depending on the project, gauge can be crucial to the fit of a knitted garment or accessory. If you need to make any size adjustments to the pattern, gauge can also help you determine how much and where to incorporate the adjustment.

Standard Yarn Weight System

Yarn Weight Symbol & Category Names	0 Lace	1 Super Fine	2 Fine	3 Light	4 Medium	5 Bulky	6 Super Bulky
Type of Yarns in Category	Fingering, 10-count crochet thread	Sock, Fingering, Baby	Sport, Baby	DK, Light Worsted	Worsted, Afghan, Aran	Chunky, Craft, Rug	Bulky, Roving

Source: Craft Yarn Council of America's www.YarnStandards.com

Needles

Just how do you go about choosing the right type of knitting needle for your project? Does it really make a difference? Everyone has their favorites when it comes to needles. Every once in a while, you should use a new needle as an excuse to get out of your comfort zone and try something different; you might just find a new favorite. Personal preference is important, but different types of needles are better suited for certain types of knitting and certain types of yarn.

Metal

Once you've been knitting a while, speed may become more important to you. Metal needles allow the yarn to slide smoothly and quickly off the needle. Also, if your yarn is multistranded or snags easily, a slick, metal needle is likely the best pick for your project.

Wood

If the yarn you're using is solid in structure, and you're doing a multicolored piece, try using wooden needles. While warm and soothing to the touch, a bamboo needle is somewhat slower to knit with than metal. However, its slowness makes it perfect for working slip stitch, when you don't want the stitches sliding off the needles too easily.

With the growing use of circular needles, many companies are now making these needles in a circular version as well.

Circular

Many knitters enjoy being able to knit with the right side of their work showing at all times. This is precisely what happens on a circular needle since you don't have to turn your piece and work the wrong side. Seeing the right side as you work can simplify a complicated color pattern. Another benefit of knitting with a circular needle is that your knitting lies comfortably in your lap as you work, putting less strain on your wrists and elbows.

Circular needles can be used just as easily for straight knitting as for circular knitting. Without joining the two knitting ends, simply knit to the end of the row, turn your piece so the wrong side is facing you, and work back across the row. For even more flexibility, you may want to invest in a set of interchangeable needles that allows you to switch between multiple needle sizes.

Knitting Needle Size Conversion Chart

METRIC (mm)	US	UK/ CANADIAN
2.0	0	14
2.25	1	13
2.75	2	12
3.0	—	11
3.25	3	10
3.5	4	—
3.75	5	9
4.0	6	8
4.5	7	7
5.0	8	6
5.5	9	5
6.0	10	4
6.5	10½	3
7.0	—	2
7.5	—	1
8.0	11	0
9.0	13	00
10.0	15	000
12.0	17	—
16.0	19	—
19.0	35	—
25.0	50	—

Other Knitting Supplies & Tools

Starting a new accessory project is easy when your knitting bag is stocked with the tools that make each part of the knitting process successful. Keeping a well-equipped knitting bag will also help you get an immediate start on your project. In fact, we suggest that you have one bag stocked and ready for your at-home knitting and another bag all set for knitting projects on the go. Along with a good selection of yarn and needles, we recommend keeping the following supplies in your knitting bag at all times.

Tape Measure: You'll need to periodically measure your work as you knit. You may also need to measure the person you are knitting for to ensure an accurate fit.

Calculator: A calculator is indispensable when you are trying to make sure your measurements match those of the pattern. It will also come in handy if you need to resize a pattern.

Small Notepad and Pens/Pencils: A notebook will help you keep track of things such as measurements, yarn amounts, dye lots, or any revisions you've made to a pattern. It's a good idea to keep an accurate record as you work your project, since it can be hard to remember that information later.

Graph Paper: We like to use graph paper to visualize color changes and stitches for a complex pattern, or to catch an inspiration before it can get away.

Gauge Ruler: A gauge ruler is very important for creating a project that matches your pattern. You should always knit a swatch and measure the gauge, adjusting your needle size if necessary.

Stitch Holders: These can be used to place stitches until you're ready to work them. Stitch holders generally come in 4- or 6-inch (10.2 or 15.2 cm) lengths. Having a couple of each size in your bag is a good idea. When sliding stitches on and off stitch holders, be sure to slide them without twisting the stitch.

Large-Eye Sewing Needle/Tapestry Needle: Besides being well suited for embroidery or embellishment work, these needles are great for sewing seams and pockets, and for weaving in yarn ends.

Stitch Markers: Stitch markers make it easy to visually keep track of your stitches. These handy little clips keep you from having to count and recount your stitches.

Cable Needle: Shorter and pointed at both ends, a cable needle is a necessity for many textured stitches and, thankfully, rather inexpensive.

Size F or G Crochet Hook: This medium-sized crochet hook works well for adding edging to projects. It can also be used to crochet chains for bag and purse ties.

Small Scissors: A small but necessary item, scissors make clipping your yarn ends quick and easy.

Zippered Pouch: We recommend using a small, clear zippered pouch to hold all the little items in your knitting bag. A pouch will keep your supplies all together, preventing them from getting lost or snagging your yarn.

Design Options

Once you've picked the perfect yarn and gathered your supplies, you've still got several decisions to make before you start knitting. Color patterns, fun edging, and cool embellishments are all great ways to tailor your knitted projects for that special little someone.

COLOR ME...BRIGHT AND CHEERFUL

Children love color. If you want to test this theory, take your young companion into a local yarn shop and see which color they pick up first. Chances are they'll go directly to the brighter, bolder color palettes. As you select yarn and colors for your project, think like a kid and keep it bright and cheerful.

We recommend that you stick to your pattern for yarn suggestions, stitch gauge, and needle size, but we also encourage a little color experimentation. Here are several techniques that will add a little or a lot of color to your knitting.

Striping

A little touch of striping will add a lot of style and variety to your knitted piece. Stripes have endless possibilities. They may be used as an allover pattern, worked in multiple colors, or serve as a simple accent on a sleeve. To incorporate a stripe in a different color, it's easiest to add the new yarn color at the beginning of a right-side row.

1. To create a stripe, drop the first color at the right-hand edge of the row.

2. Pick up the new color, and lay it next to the edge in position to be used, leaving a 3- to 6-inch (7.6 to 15.2 cm) tail.

3. Proceed to the end of the row. Turn work.

If you purl this new color back to the right side edge of your piece, you have added a row and widened the stripe. In stockinette stitch, the new color will lie flat and be an accent stripe to the main color. Follow your pattern instructions for information on how wide to make the stripe and when to return to the original color.

Intarsia

Intarsia is used to work small, self-contained designs within a larger piece of knitting. When you see hearts, boats, and stars adorning children's garments, you're seeing an example of intarsia. Intarsia designs are often graphed or charted and have specific instructions regarding how and where they are to be placed. The basic technique involves crossing yarns, and switching yarn colors, by linking them on the backside of the work.

1. Following your pattern, work to the color change.

2. Pick up yarn of the new color from under the previously worked yarn.

3. Pull the new yarn up and over the dropped yarn, and work your next stitch with the new color.

Tip

When you cross the yarn to change colors, pay attention to how loosely or how tightly you have intertwined this yarn—not too loose so that it creates a hole and not so tight that it distorts the design. Make a conscious effort to keep this tension even, and always cross the yarns on the backside of your work.

4. Across a small area, as you work with the new color, carry the old color across the back loosely so it doesn't distort your knitted piece.

5. If you are working a larger design, bobbins of yarn are frequently used rather than carrying the yarn across the back.

6. When it is time to go back to the old color of yarn, simply drop the new yarn and come from underneath with the main color yarn. Adjust the stitch tension, and finish your row.

Charts Made Simple

A knitting necessity, charts are a visual method of transmitting simple information. With just one look at a chart, you'll see a picture that would take a thousand words to explain in "knit-ese." Reading charts is simple, although somewhat contrary to what you learned in school about reading.

To explain the basics, here is an easy-to-follow example:

This Pumpkin design will take the space of 13 rows and 12 stitches. Your pattern should give you the placement to begin your design.

Working in the traditional back-and-forth, right-and-wrong-side manner, you would proceed as follows: As you begin working RS Row #1, start at the bottom right corner of the graph and work the stitches from right to left across the row. For Row #2, read across from left to right, working the stitches as indicated. For RS Row #3, work the stitches as shown from right to left. Repeat until you've worked all of the rows and stitches in the chart.

Note: The exception to these instructions will be the knitter or pattern that works a project from the top down. Unless the charts have been altered, you'll need to reverse your thinking and work the graph from the top to the bottom.

Slip Stitch

This technique may give you the best color mixture with the least amount of effort. Slip stitch patterns work only one color in a row at a time, although your pattern may provide specific instructions regarding yarn color and which stitches to slip. To slip a stitch, you simply move the stitch from the right-hand needle to the left-hand needle without working it.

On the right side of your work, all stitches are slipped as if to purl (purlwise) unless instructed differently. In slip stitch, the wrong-side row is usually worked across in a purl stitch.

By working your piece in rows of different colors and by slipping some of the stitches from the preceding row onto your current working needle, a pattern will evolve. This is a very easy way to mix up a lot of colors and create an eye-catching garment.

Note: If you're looking for texture and density rather than vivid color, try working a slip stitch pattern in a monochromatic piece.

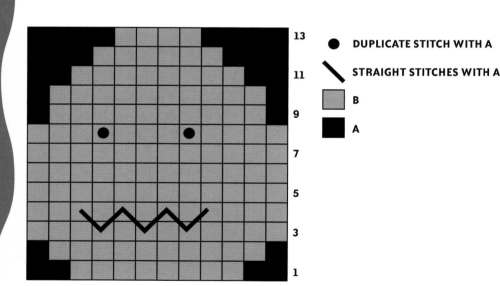

● **DUPLICATE STITCH WITH A**

╲ **STRAIGHT STITCHES WITH A**

▨ **B**

■ **A**

EDGINGS

Adding extra flair to your project is easy with exciting, textured edgings, and you've got lots to choose from. Children in particular seem to enjoy these little additions, so add edgings to your accessories anytime they might be appropriate. Edgings are also a great way to add a contrasting yarn, or even a bit of more expensive novelty yarn, to your project. This way you can get a great one-of-a-kind look without breaking the bank.

When working on a child's project, make sure you keep the edging in proportion to the rest of the project, in both size and style. You don't want the edging trim to overwhelm the project itself. But our best advice is to be creative and have some fun with your edgings: think "over the edge"!

Fringe

Although your fringe can be any length, most scarves and shawls use fringe that is 3 to 5 inches (7.6 to 12.7 cm) long. Your decision on length will depend in part on how well your yarn drapes or hangs. Also take into account the age of the person wearing or using the item: generally speaking, the smaller the child, the shorter the fringe. Before you get started, you'll want to figure out how many tassels you want and decide the spacing of each one so that they are evenly placed.

1. Cut several lengths of yarn (four to six pieces) twice as long as the desired length of the fringe, and then fold the pieces in half.

2. Using a crochet hook, feed the looped end of your yarn pieces through a secure place on the edge of your knitted piece.

3. Once you have fed the looped end through, take the cut ends of yarn and work them through the loop. Pull the ends securely, and repeat the process for the next tassel.

4. When you have finished making all of your tassels, trim the ends evenly to your desired length.

Pom-Poms

Pom-poms have passed the test of time and make lively edging for children's scarves, ponchos, and hats. They can be created from one yarn or from multiple yarns in fun colors. To make one, you'll need a piece of sturdy cardboard or plastic (we like to use a compact disc case) and these simple steps:

1. Wind the yarn around a compact disc case (or whatever you are using) multiple times. The more times you wind, the fuller, and better looking, the pom-pom becomes.

2. After you have wound enough yarn, cut a separate 10-inch (25.4 cm) strand of yarn. As you carefully slide the yarn off the case, tightly tie the strand around the yarn, forming the center of the pom-pom. Do not cut the yarn tails yet.

Tip

If you don't have a lot of yarn left over from your project, consider adding a coordinating color.

3. Standing over a wastebasket, carefully trim the ends of your pom-pom, shaping them as you trim. You can make your pom-pom as big or as small as you want. Bigger pom-poms will look floppier.

4. After you have made your pom-poms, use 10-inch (25.4 cm) strands to secure the pom-poms to your garment.

5. Weave in the ends of these tails and trim them close to the wrong side of your work.

Note: There are professional pom-pom makers on the market, so, if you find yourself needing a lot of pom-poms, you may want to invest in one.

Ruffles

Ruffles are a popular way to add a feminine touch to any hand-knit project. There are many varieties of ruffles. They can be worked in almost any stitch, although depending on the yarn you're using, your ruffle will likely drape better with a flatter stitch. There are basically two ways to create this type of edging, depending on whether you start or end with the ruffle.

If you start your project with a ruffle, your instructions will have you cast on three or four times the number of stitches you'll ultimately need for your project. You'll work your ruffle for the instructed length and then decrease your stitches—usually by knitting or purling two or three together—every stitch along one or maybe two rows. This will leave you with a ruffled edge and the correct number of stitches for the body of your project on the needle.

If you're creating your ruffle at the end of your project, you will work the body of your project and then increase two or three stitches into each stitch along one row. You'll then be able to work the ruffle in almost any stitch you want until you reach your desired length. To finish the ruffle, bind off the way you normally would, either in a pattern stitch, a knit stitch, or a purl stitch.

. . . .

Tip
Adding ruffles to the end of a project is a great way to add length to an item a child is outgrowing.

. . . .

Lizzie Loops

Children are sure to enjoy this super-cool edging technique. What's more, these loops are really fast and easy to accomplish, the perfect addition to the top edge of a purse. Unlike some loop stitches that are "knit in," these loops are created with a long tail of yarn and a crochet hook.

1. Working from front to back along the edge of your project and using a crochet hook, pull the yarn (usually directly from the ball of yarn) through one of the edge stitches, creating a loop at each side of the edge stitch.

2. Tie the two loops into a single knot.

3. Move to the next edge stitch, repeating this process across the entire edge of the project.

Tip

If you're having trouble holding the strap and braiding it at the same time, tape the knotted end to a flat surface while you work.

Braided Strap

You've got a lot of options when it comes to straps, but this simple braid is both easy and durable. With a stylish twist design, it's sure to please even the youngest fashion critic.

1. Working with a single color or a two-color combination of yarn, cut eight lengths of yarn according to your pattern instructions. Gather the eight strands together and knot one end, leaving extra at the knotted end. Separate the strands into four double strands.

2. Pull the center double strands straight towards you. Using photo 1 as a guide, loop the right-side double strands out to the right and cross over the center strands.

3. With the left-side double strands, loop out to the left, crossing over the right-side strands and under the center strands, and then passing through the loop created by the right-side strands (photo 2).

4. Pull both outside strands tightly while holding the center strands taut as shown in photo 3.

5. Continue this process until the strap reaches the desired length.

Note: You may switch the inside and outside strands either to equalize the length or to create a color pattern.

Ribbing

Ribbed edges are probably the most common edging used by the hand knitter. Not only do they give a great finished look to an edge, ribbing also creates elasticity that makes it a great choice for waistbands, necklines, and sleeve cuffs.

The most common rib is the knit 1, purl 1 stitch rib. The key to creating a rib stitch is that you need to keep the knit stitches and purl stitches going up your rows in sequence. If you're working in the round, keep knitting all your knit stitches and purling your purl stitches. If you're working back and forth on the needle, you'll have to pay attention to your stitches to see the knits and the purls. Most patterns will give you row-by-row instructions.

There are many variations on the basic rib. Try doing a knit 2, purl 2 rib or a knit 3, purl 1 rib. Ribs can even be created with small cables worked into them.

EMBELLISHMENTS

Beads, buttons, and fancy embroidery stitches can add the perfect touch of style and creativity to your project without making the knitting steps more complicated. Consider using one of these methods to spice up an otherwise plain piece or to create that unique, custom project.

Beading

You can add beads in one of two ways. Beads can either be strung on the yarn and then knit into the project, or they can be stitched on after your project is complete. Whichever method you choose to use, beading can add a real flourish to your knitting, and be fun along the way.

Beads come in many varieties, so you have lots of choices. Before making your selections, you'll need to consider the final use of your project. Do the beads you choose have to be washable? If you choose glass beads, is there a chance they'll break? Are you going to want to change the beads or take them off? Let the type of project you're making, and the type of yarn and beads you are using, dictate the approach you choose.

Knitting beads into your project is the sturdiest beading option. This method works best for fairly simple projects, with simple bead designs, and with yarns that allow for easy bead stringing. First, you'll have to calculate how many beads your design requires and your total yardage of yarn. Divide by the number of skeins to determine how many beads to string onto each skein of yarn. Once you've done your math, string the beads onto the yarn before you start, and, as you work, slide a bead into your knitting each time your pattern calls for one.

If your beading pattern is very complex, it might be easier to add beads after the piece is knit. This method also allows for easy corrections, should you make a mistake. To stitch a bead in place, use a long strand of yarn that matches the background of your knitting; you may need to divide multistrand yarn into thinner strands. Using a running stitch along the wrong side of your work, secure each bead in its proper place on the right side of your knitting. Try to work neatly, without leaving long exposed stretches of yarn on the wrong side that could snag and pull. After every bead is secured, securely stitch the tail of yarn to the wrong side before moving on to the next bead. As you work, lay out your piece occasionally, right side up, and make sure you have no puckering.

Buttons

Buttons aren't just for closures anymore. Try using these fun fixtures as a creative way to embellish your knitting. Buttons can really add a lot of color and flavor to your projects, especially children's garments and accessories. They're usually washable, relatively inexpensive, and easy to use.

Have your little one put his or her special fingerprint on a hand-knit item by letting them pick the accent button or buttons. And later, if you want to change the look, there's no need to rip out your knitting; just remove and replace the button. What could be easier?

Take a look at our Button Belt (page 50) and Bag (page 90) for some good ideas on how to use buttons. For the Button Belt, we used very plain but colorful buttons to jazz up a relatively simple accessory. This technique kept the knitting project quick and easy, but gave us an end result that was fun and creative, with that unique look kids want in their wardrobe. Buttons make it easy to create coordinating accessories—another thing kids love—like the bag project.

Embroidery Stitches

Very few knitters think of their hand knits as a place to do embroidery, but why not? Young ones will love the details embroidery stitches provide, especially over areas of plain knitting. And you almost always have enough yarn left over from your knitting to add these little extras, such as a Lazy Daisy or a French Knot (see page 108).

To create these simple embroidery stitches, the only supplies you need are a long tail of yarn and a tapestry needle. Work the embroidery stitches as you would regular embroidery, paying careful attention to the holes in your knitting. When possible, place your tapestry needle in the firmest area of your work.

Also, make sure you don't pull the yarn too tightly across the wrong side of your work. You want your work to remain smooth, but you don't want long strands of loose yarn that could get caught on something. To avoid these kinds of issues, try to keep the wrong side of your work as neat as possible.

If you're creating a large area of embroidery, we recommend drawing out your design on a piece of graph paper, using the lines on the graph paper to represent stitches and rows. This will help you determine how to lay out the design over your knitting. When you're ready to start your embroidery, start in the middle of the design and the knitting, and work outward.

Abbreviations

Approx	approximately		rep	repeat
beg	begin(ning)		rnd(s)	round(s)
BO	bind off		RS	right side of work
cn	cable needle		sl st	slip stitch
CO	cast on		ssk	slip 1 knitwise, slip 1 knitwise, K2 slipped stitches together through back loop - 1 decrease has been made
cont	continue			
ctr	center			
dec	decreas(e)(ing)(ed)			
dpn	double-pointed needle		st(s)	stitch(es)
est	establish(ed)		St st	stockinette stitch
EOR	every other row		Tbl	through back loop
foll	follow(ing)		tog	together
inc	increas(e)(ing)		WS	wrong side of work or garment
K or k	knit			
k2tog	knit 2 together		wyib	with yarn in back of work
LH	left hand		wyif	with yarn in front of work
P or p	purl		X	time(s)
p2tog	purl 2 together		Yd	yard
patt	pattern		YO	yarn over needle to make a new stitch
psso	pass slip stitch over last stitch worked			
PU	pick up stitches		( )	work directions as a group as many times as indicated
RH	right hand		*	asterisks, starting point for repeating directions as many times as indicated
rem	remain(ing)(s)			

Projects

Rib-It! Mittens

SKILL LEVEL

Intermediate

SIZES

Small (Medium)

FINISHED MEASUREMENTS

Length 6½ (7)"/17 (18)cm, with cuff folded in half

MATERIALS AND TOOLS

Approx total: 660yd/594m of (4) worsted weight yarn, superwash wool
Color A: 220yd/198m of (4) worsted weight yarn, superwash wool, in lime green
Color B: 220yd/198m of (4) worsted weight yarn, superwash wool, in aqua
Color C: 220yd/198m of (4) worsted weight yarn, superwash wool, in yellow
Knitting needles: 4mm (size 6 U.S.) *or size to obtain gauge*
Tapestry needle

GAUGE

24 sts and 40 rows = 4"/10cm in Linked Stripe Stitch
24 sts and 26 rows = 4"/10cm in Garter Stitch (knit every row)
Always take time to check your gauge.

SPECIAL ABBREVIATION

Make one stitch (M1): Pick up the horizontal strand lying between the stitch just worked and the next stitch; knit the newly picked up stitch through the back loop (increase made).

Aren't these fun mittens perfect

PATTERN STITCH

LINKED STRIPE STITCH multiple of 4sts/16 row repeat

Row 1 (RS): Knit.

Row 2: Knit.

Row 3: K1, *sl 2 wyib, k2; repeat from * to last 3 sts, sl 2, k1.

Row 4: P1, *sl 2 wyif, p2; repeat from * to last 3 sts, sl 2, p1.

Rows 5–8: Repeat rows 1–4.

Rows 9 and 10: Knit.

Row 11: K1, *sl 2 wyib, k2; repeat from * to last 3 sts, sl 2, k1.

Row 12: P1, *sl 2 wyif, p2; repeat from * to last 3 sts, sl 2, p1.

Rows 13 and 14: Knit.

Rows 15 and 16: Repeat rows 11 and 12.

Repeat rows 1–16 for pattern.

Left Mitten

CUFF

With C, cast on 36 (40) sts.

Work in Garter Stitch until piece measures 3 (3½)"/8 (9)cm from beginning. End with a RS row.

BODY

Next row (WS): With B, purl.

Work rows 1–16 of Linked Stripe Stitch.

for paddycakes?

SHAPE THUMB

Row 1 (RS): K14 (16), M1, k2, M1, k20 (22)—38 (42) sts.

Row 2 (WS): Knit.

Row 3: K14 (16), M1, k4, M1, k20 (22)—40 (44) sts.

Row 4: Knit.

Row 5: K14 (16), M1, k6, M1, k20 (22)—42 (46) sts.

Row 6: Knit.

Row 7 (start thumb): K22 (24), turn, cast on 1 st, k9, turn, cast on 1 st, k10, place marker and leave remaining 20 (22) sts on needle unworked.

Work 9 (11) rows in Garter Stitch over the 10 thumb sts (for total of 10 [12] rows of thumb).

Next row (RS): K2tog across thumb sts—5 sts.

Cut yarn and thread it through the remaining 5 sts. Pull tightly to secure. Sew thumb seam.

CONTINUE BODY

With RS facing, rejoin yarn at right side base of thumb (next to the sts that have already been worked on the right-hand needle); pick up 6 sts around base of thumb and continue across the unworked sts—40 (44) sts on needle.

Next row (WS): Knit.

Beginning with row 3, work 16 (20) rows in Linked Stripe Stitch, decrease 1 st in last row—39 (43) sts.

SHAPE TOP

Row 1 (RS): K1, k2tog, k14 (16), k2tog tbl, k1, k2tog, k14 (16), k2tog tbl, k1—35 (39) sts.

Row 2 and all WS rows: Knit.

Row 3: K1, k2tog, k12 (14), k2tog tbl, k1, k2tog, k12 (14), k2tog tbl, k1—31 (35) sts.

Row 5: K1, k2tog, k10 (12), k2tog tbl, k1, k2tog, k10 (12), k2tog tbl, k1—27 (31) sts.

Row 7: K1, k2tog, k8 (10), k2tog tbl, k1, k2tog, k8 (10), k2tog tbl, k1—23 (27) sts.

Row 9: K1, k2tog, k6 (8), k2tog tbl, k1, k2tog, k6 (8), k2tog tbl, k1—19 (23) sts.

Row 11: K1, k2tog, k4 (6), k2tog tbl, k1, k2tog, k4 (6), k2tog tbl, k1—15 (19) sts.

For "small" size—discontinue knitting and bind off sts.

Row 13: K1, k2tog, k2 (4), k2tog tbl, k1, k2tog, k2 (4), k2tog tbl, k1—11 (15) sts.

Row 15: K1, k2tog, k0 (2), k2tog tbl, k1, k2tog, k0 (2), k2tog tbl, k1—7 (11) sts.

Bind off, leaving a long tail to sew side seam.

Right Mitten

Work as for left mitten to thumb shaping, using C for cuff and A for body.

SHAPE THUMB

Row 1 (RS): K20 (22), M1, k2, M1, k14 (16)—38 (42) sts.

Row 2 (WS): Knit.

Row 3: K20 (22), M1, k4, M1, k14 (16)—40 (44) sts.

Row 4: Knit.

Row 5: K20 (22), M1, k6, M1, k14 (16)—42 (46) sts.

Row 6: Knit.

Row 7 (start thumb): K28 (30), turn, cast on 1 st, k9, turn, cast on 1 st, k10, place marker and leave remaining 14 (16) sts on needle unworked.

Work 9 (11) rows in Garter Stitch over the 10 thumb sts (for total of 10 [12] rows).

Next row (RS): K2tog across thumb sts—5 sts.

Cut yarn and thread it through the remaining 5 sts. Pull tightly to secure. Sew thumb seam.

CONTINUE BODY AND SHAPE TOP

Complete right mitten as for left mitten.

FINISHING

Weave in ends on wrong sides of mittens. Fold mittens in half and sew side seams. Fold cuff over.

This project was knit with:

• •

Cascade Yarns' 220 Superwash, worsted weight, 100% superwash wool, 3.5oz/ 100g = approx 220yd/198m per ball

(A) 1 ball, color #851

(B) 1 ball, color #849

(C) 1 ball, color #820

Rib-It! Hat

Oh me. Oh my! There's a hat in the sky!

MATERIALS AND TOOLS

Approx total: 660yd/594m of [4] worsted
    weight yarn, superwash wool
Color A: 220yd/198m of [4] worsted
    weight yarn, superwash wool, in
    lime green
Color B: 220yd/198m of [4] worsted
    weight yarn, superwash wool, in aqua
Color C: 220yd/198m of [4] worsted
    weight yarn, superwash wool, in yellow
Knitting needles: 4mm (size 6 U.S.) straight
    needles and set of 4 double-pointed
    needles *or size to obtain gauge*
Crochet hook
Tapestry needle

GAUGE

24 sts and 40 rows = 4"/10cm in Linked
    Stripe Stitch
Always take time to check your gauge.

PATTERN STITCH

LINKED STRIPE STITCH

Row 1 (RS): With A, knit.

Row 2: With A, knit.

Row 3: With B, k1, *sl 2 wyib, k2; repeat
from * to last 3 sts, sl 2, k1.

Row 4: With B, p1, *sl 2 wyif, p2; repeat
from * to last 3 sts, sl 2, p1.

Rows 5–8: Repeat rows 1–4.

Rows 9 and 10: With B, knit.

Row 11: With A, k1, *sl 2 wyib,
k2; repeat from * to last
3 sts, sl 2, k1.

Row 12: With A, p1, *sl 2 wyif, p2; repeat
from * to last 3 sts, sl 2, p1.

Rows 13 and 14: With B, knit.

Rows 15 and 16 with Color A: Repeat
rows 11 and 12.

Repeat rows 1–16
for pattern.

Hat

BRIM

Note: The hat is worked in rows until crown shaping.

With C, cast on 108 (120) sts.

Work 11 (13) rows in Garter Stitch (knit every row).

BODY

Work Linked Stripe Stitch until hat measures 5½ (7)"/14 (18)cm from beginning.

CROWN

With RS facing, redistribute sts evenly on 3 double-pointed needles with 36 (40) sts per needle.

Round 1 (RS): With B, *p12, place marker; repeat from * around. Place a marker to indicate the beginning of the round. Join to work sts in the round.

Round 2: With C, *k10, k2tog; repeat from * around—99 (110) sts.

Round 3: With C, purl.

Round 4: With A, *k9, k2tog; repeat from * around—90 (100) sts.

Round 5: With A, purl.

Round 6: With B, *k8, k2tog; repeat from * around—81 (90) sts.

Round 7: With B, purl.

Round 8: With C, *k7, k2tog; repeat from * around—72 (80) sts.

Round 9: With C, purl.

Round 10: With A, *k6, k2tog; repeat from * around—63 (70) sts.

Round 11: With A, purl, decrease 1 st (p2tog) in small size only—62 (70) sts.

Round 12: With B, k2tog around—31 (35) sts.

Round 13: With B, purl, decrease 1 st (p2tog)—30 (34) sts.

Round 14: With C, k2tog around—15 (17) sts.

Round 15: With C, purl.

Round 16: With A, knit.

Round 17: With A, purl.

Cut yarn leaving a long tail. With tapestry needle, weave tail through remaining stitches, slide stitches off the needle, and pull yarn tightly to gather top of hat. Weave end into wrong side of hat. Sew back hat seam, taking care to match the color striping as you sew.

EARFLAPS (OPTIONAL)

From back seam, fold hat in half. Folded hat, measured at edge of brim should be 9 (10)"/23 (25)cm. Place marker in the middle of the brim edge, pick up and knit 9 (11) sts on both sides of marker—18 (22) sts.

Next row (WS): Knit.

Work 22 (24) rows in Linked Stripe pattern.

SHAPE EARFLAP

Row 1: With B, k2tog, sl 1, *k2, sl 2 wyib; repeat from * to last 3 sts, sl 1, k2tog—16 (20) sts.

Row 2: With B, p1, sl 1, *p2tog, sl 2 wyif; repeat from * to last 2 sts, sl 1, p1—13 (16) sts.

Row 3: With B, k2tog, knit to last 2 sts, k2tog—11 (14) sts.

Row 4: With B, knit.

Row 5: With A, k2tog, knit to last 2 sts, k2tog—9 (12) sts.

Bind off as if to knit.

Repeat for other earflap.

FINISHING

With crochet hook, work a row of single crochet around outside edges of earflaps. Weave in all ends on wrong side of hat.

TIES

With one strand each of A and B, and 2 double-pointed needles, cast on 2 sts. Make two I-cords, 16"/41cm long. Ties may also be braided or use any method of your choosing.

POM-POM

With C, make a pom-pom as described on page 17. Secure pom-pom to top of hat.

Note: See page 104 for information on making I-cord.

This project was knit with:
• •

Cascade Yarns' 220 Superwash, worsted weight, 100% superwash wool, 3.5oz/ 100g = approx 220yd/198m per ball

(A) 1 ball, color #851
(B) 1 ball, color #849
(C) 1 ball, color #820

Leo the Lion

SKILL LEVEL

Intermediate

FINISHED MEASUREMENTS

Lion 7"/18cm tall x 11"/28cm long seated, excluding tail
Head approximately 4"/10cm in all dimensions

MATERIALS AND TOOLS

Approx total: 392yd/353m of  DK weight yarn, cotton
Color A: 196yd/176m of ❸ DK weight yarn, cotton, in light orange
Color B: 98yd/88m of ❸ DK weight yarn, cotton, in dark orange
Color C: 98yd/88m of ❸ DK weight yarn, cotton, in yellow
Knitting needles: 4.5mm (size 7 U.S.) *or size to obtain gauge*
Tapestry needle
Polyester fiberfill (washable)

GAUGE

16 sts and 20 rows = 4"/10cm in Stockinette Stitch (knit on RS, purl on WS)
Always take time to check your gauge.

Leo helps me

Lion

With A, cast on 80 sts.

Work in Stockinette Stitch until piece measures 4"/10cm from beginning. End with a WS row.

SHAPE LEGS

Row 1 (RS): Bind off first 15 sts, knit remaining sts—65 sts.

Row 2: Bind off first 15 sts, purl remaining sts—50 sts.

BODY

Work even in Stockinette Stitch until piece measures 7"/18cm from beginning. End with a WS row.

LEGS

Row 1 (RS): K50, cast on 15 sts at end of row—65 sts.

Row 2 (WS): P65, cast on 15 sts at end of row—80 sts.

Work even in Stockinette Stitch until piece measures 11"/28cm from beginning.

Bind off, leaving a long yarn tail for seaming.

With yarn needle and yarn tail, sew a running stitch around all edges of the head piece. Pull gently on the yarn tail to form a pouch, fill the pouch with fiberfill as you pull the yarn tail tight. When pouch is completely closed and full of fiberfill, tie off the back and sew the head to the body of the lion.

be brave—even in the dark.

HEAD

With A, cast on 60 sts.

Work in Stockinette Stitch until piece measures 8"/20cm from beginning. Bind off, leaving a long yarn tail for seaming.

FINISHING

Lightly block the body and head. Lay body of lion out flat. Fold in half lengthwise, with right sides together. With yarn tail, sew one side seam to form lower edge of lion (from fold to leg). When sewing lower edge, create a small gusset where tail will attach. Fold back legs in half and sew each leg seam. Sew each front leg seam. Sew underbelly seam. Turn body of lion right side out. Lightly block lion again if needed. Stuff body with fiberfill.

MANE

Holding all three colors together, create the loop embellishment around the head and face of lion.

Note: See page 18 for more information on Lizzie loops.

FACE

With B, embroider French Knot eyes and overstitch the nose and mouth to create the lion face.

Note: See page 108 for information on French Knots.

TAIL

Cut two 14"/36cm lengths of all three colors. Thread all six strands through the bottom of the lion at tail gusset. Fold strands in half then divide the strands in 3 groups of 2 strands each. Braid the tail and tie off the end. Trim tail.

This project was knit with:

Skacel's Schulana Merino Cotton, DK weight, 53% wool/47% cotton, 1.75oz/50g = approx 98yd/88m per ball

(A) 2 balls, color #31
(B) 1 ball, color #9
(C) 1 ball, color #5

Sleepover Slippers

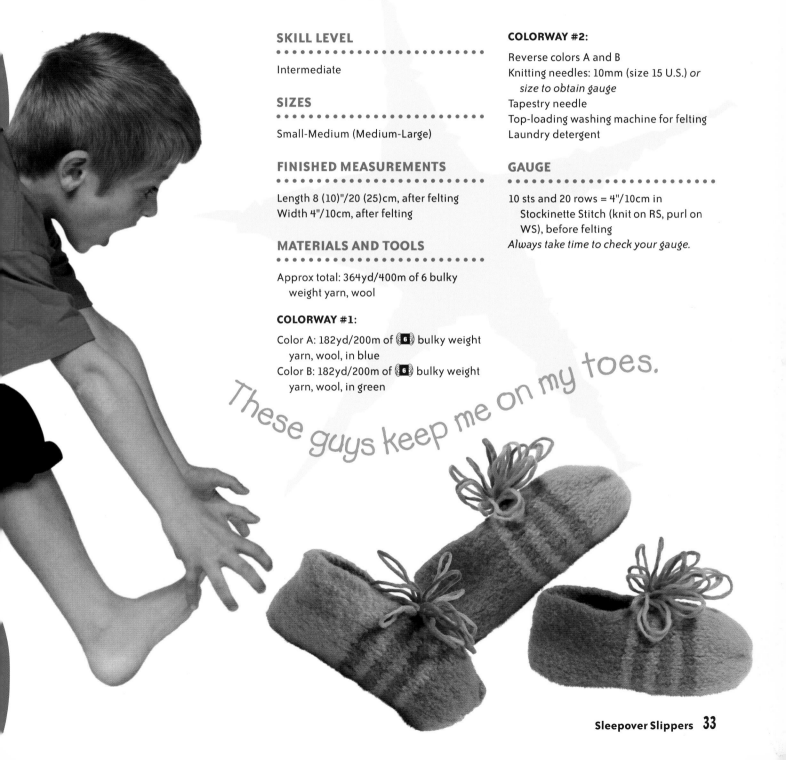

SKILL LEVEL

Intermediate

SIZES

Small-Medium (Medium-Large)

FINISHED MEASUREMENTS

Length 8 (10)"/20 (25)cm, after felting
Width 4"/10cm, after felting

MATERIALS AND TOOLS

Approx total: 364yd/400m of 6 bulky
   weight yarn, wool

COLORWAY #1:

Color A: 182yd/200m of (6) bulky weight
   yarn, wool, in blue
Color B: 182yd/200m of (6) bulky weight
   yarn, wool, in green

COLORWAY #2:

Reverse colors A and B
Knitting needles: 10mm (size 15 U.S.) *or
   size to obtain gauge*
Tapestry needle
Top-loading washing machine for felting
Laundry detergent

GAUGE

10 sts and 20 rows = 4"/10cm in
   Stockinette Stitch (knit on RS, purl on
   WS), before felting
Always take time to check your gauge.

These guys keep me on my toes.

Slipper (make 2)

Note: You may work both slippers in the same colorway, or work each slipper in a different colorway.

With A, cast on 36 (36) sts.

Work 18 (23) rows in Stockinette Stitch.

BEGIN STRIPING

Continue Stockinette Stitch in the following color sequence: *2 rows B, 2 rows A; repeat from * 2 more times.

With B, continue Stockinette Stitch until slipper measures 10 (12½)"/25 (32)cm from beginning.

Note: Your slippers should shrink about 2"/5cm in length in the felting process.

Bind off as follows: k2tog (keep stitch on right needle),* k2tog; bind off these 2 sts; repeat from * across row until all sts are bound off.

FINISHING

Fold slipper in half with right sides facing out. Sew toe edge seam carefully without creating a seam selvage. Run the yarn tail through the seam to gather. Secure so that the toe is gathered closed. Weave in yarn tail on wrong side of slipper. Sew heel seam.

Sew top half of slipper, from toe to striped section, leaving approximately 4 (4½)"/10 (11)cm open at heel end.

FELTING

Place assembled slippers into a lingerie bag or pillowcase. Set the washing machine for a small load and fill with hot water. Add detergent. Also add a large old towel and/or a pair of jeans for additional agitation. Do not add anything that will create fuzz or bleed color. Run your washing machine, stopping to check progress periodically. You do not want the slippers to over felt and get too small. When the slippers have felted enough, you can either take them out of the machine and rinse them in cold water by hand or let them run through the spin cycle with cold water. During the felting process, as you shape your slippers you can stretch and pull them slightly, shaping them to best fit the wearer's foot. Then lay the slippers out flat to dry.

Note: A top-loading washing machine must be used for machine felting. Front loading machines do not create the agitation needed to complete the process.

LIZZIE LOOP EMBELLISHMENT

To create the loopy embellishment, use several yards of A and a tapestry needle. Make two loops and then tie each pair of loops into a knot. Repeat with B. Be sure to add the loops after the slippers are felted.

Note: See page 18 for more information on making Lizzie loops.

Design Tip

Unsure how the yarn you are using will felt? Knit a swatch as recommended in the pattern and then felt your swatch! Not only can you check out your knitting gauge, you can also see just how the yarn will felt.

This project was knit with:

Skacel's Loft, bulky weight, 100% merino wool, 1.75oz/50g = approx 91yd/100m per ball
(A) 2 balls, color #1239
(B) 2 balls, color #1238

Loot Bags

Trick or Treat.

SKILL LEVEL

Intermediate

FINISHED MEASUREMENTS

Bag 10 x 13"/25 x 33cm, excluding handle
Handle 22"/56cm

MATERIALS AND TOOLS

Approx total: 660yd/594m of (4) worsted
   weight yarn, superwash wool
Color A: 220yd/198m of (4) worsted
   weight yarn, superwash wool, in black
Color B: 220yd/198m of (4) worsted
   weight yarn, superwash wool,
   in orange
Color C: 220yd/198m of (4)
   worsted weight yarn,
   superwash wool, in white
Knitting needles: 5mm (size 8
   U.S.) or size to obtain gauge
Tapestry needle

GAUGE

18 sts and 24 rows = 4"/10cm in
   Stockinette Stitch (knit on RS,
   purl on WS)
Always take time to check
   your gauge.

Give me something good to eat.

PATTERN STITCH

SEED STITCH

Row 1: *K1, p1; repeat from * to end.
Row 2: *P1, k1; repeat from * to end.
Repeat rows 1 and 2 for pattern.

Bag

With A, cast on 62 sts.

Work 3 rows in Seed Stitch.

Work even in Stockinette Stitch until piece measures 13"/33cm from beginning.

Begin working chart #1 or chart #2 (page 38).

Note: Details of pumpkin face or skeleton face is overstitched on pumpkin or skull after bag is knit.

Continue in Stockinette Stitch until piece measures 19½"/50cm from beginning.

Work 3 rows in Seed Stitch. Bind off in Seed Stitch pattern.

HANDLE

With A, cast on 7 sts.

Row 1: K1, *p1, k1; repeat from * to end.

Repeat row 1 until piece measures 22"/56cm from beginning. Bind off in pattern.

FINISHING

Fold bag with right sides facing together and bringing cast-on row up to meet bind-off row. With A, sew side seams together. Turn bag right side out. Lightly block bag.

EMBROIDERY DETAILS

Chart #1: With A, duplicate stitch eyes and straight stitch mouth on pumpkin as indicated on chart.

Chart #2: With C, work French Knots at end of cross bones. With A, duplicate stitch eyes and nose as indicated on chart.

Sew one end of handle inside bag at each side seam. Take care not to twist handle.

Weave ends into wrong side of bag.

This project was knit with:

• •

Cascade Yarns' 220 Superwash, worsted weight, 100% superwash wool, 3.5oz/ 100g = approx 220yd/198m per ball
(A) 1 ball, color #815
(B) 1 ball, color #825
(C) 1 ball, color #817

● **DUPLICATE STITCH WITH A**

╲ **STRAIGHT STITCHES WITH A**

▨ **B**

■ **A**

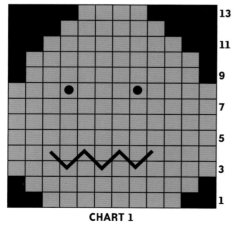

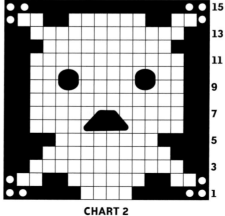

■ **A**

□ **C**

◐ **FRENCH KNOT WITH C**

● ▲ **STRAIGHT STITCHES WITH A**

13 11 9 7 5 3 1
CHART 1

15 13 11 9 7 5 3 1
CHART 2

Cable Guy Socks

SKILL LEVEL

Experienced

SIZES

Small (Large)

FINISHED MEASUREMENTS

Cuff to heel 7 (8½)"/18 (22)cm
Heel to toe 7 (8½)"/18 (22)cm

GAUGE

26 sts and 32 rows = 4"/10cm in
 Stockinette Stitch (knit every round)
Always take time to check your gauge.

Just right for coming or going.

MATERIALS AND TOOLS

Approx total: 420yd/378m of (3) DK
 weight yarn, cotton
Color A: 105yd/95m of (3) DK weight
 yarn, cotton, in green
Color B: 105yd/95m of (3) DK weight yarn,
 cotton, in brown
Color C: 105yd/95m of (3) DK weight
 yarn, cotton, in dark yellow
Color D: 105yd/95m of (3) DK weight
 yarn, cotton, cotton, in orange
Knitting needles: 3.75mm (size 5 U.S.) set
 of 4 double-pointed needles *or size to
 obtain gauge*
Stitch marker
Cable needle
Stitch holder
Tapestry needle

SPECIAL ABBREVIATIONS

Cable 4 sts back (C4B): Slip 2 sts onto cable needle and hold in back, k2, k2 from cable needle.

Cable 4 sts front (C4F): Slip 2 sts onto cable needle and hold in front, k2 sts, k2 from cable needle.

Slip, slip, knit (ssk): Slip 2 sts, one at a time, as if to knit, insert left needle into slipped sts and knit them together.

PATTERN STITCH

K1, P1 RIBBING

Round 1: *K1, p1; repeat from * around.

Repeat round 1 for pattern.

Sock (make 2)

CUFF

With B, cast on 44 (48) sts onto one double-pointed needle.

Row 1 (WS): Knit.

Row 2 (RS): *K1, p1; repeat from * across.

With RS facing, distribute sts on three double-pointed needles as follows: slip 14 sts onto needle #1, 15 (17) sts onto needle #2, and remaining 15 (17) sts onto needle #3. Join to work sts in the round; place marker between needles #1 and #3 to indicate beginning of round.

Work K1, P1 Ribbing in the following color sequence: 3 rounds with B, 3 rounds with A, 3 rounds with B, 1 round with C, 1 round with A, 2 rounds with D, 3 rounds with B.

LEG

Change to A.

Rounds 1–3: Knit.

Round 4:

Needle #1: K1, C4B, k4, C4F, k1;

Needle #2: K2, p2, k2, p2 (4), k1, C4B, k2;

Needle #3: K2, C4F, k1, p2 (4), k2, p2, k2.

Rounds 5–7: Knit.

Round 8:

Needle #1: K3, C4F, C4B, k3;

Needle #2: K2, p2, k2, p2 (4), k3, C4F;

Needle #3: C4B, k3, p2 (4), k2, p2, k2.

Rounds 9–40 (48): Repeat the first 8 rounds 4 (5) times.

Round 41 (49):

Needle #1: K1, C4B, k4, C4F, k1;

Needles #2 and #3: Knit.

Redistribute sts as follows: Slip first 4 (5) sts of needle #2 back onto needle #1, slip last 4 (5) sts of needle #3 onto needle #1. Needle #1 now holds 22 (24) sts for instep; these sts can be placed on a st holder and will be worked later. Slip all remaining sts on needles #2 and #3 onto one needle, for a total of 22 (24) sts for heel flap.

HEEL FLAP

Row 1: With WS of heel facing, attach A, sl 1, purl all remaining sts.

Row 2 (RS): *Sl 1, k1; repeat from * to end.

Row 3 (WS): Sl 1, purl remaining sts.

Rows 4–17 (19): Repeat last 2 rows in the following color sequence: 2 rows with C, 2 rows with D, 2 rows with B, 2 rows with A, 2 rows with C, 2 rows with D, 2 rows with B, (2 rows with A for larger size only).

TURN HEEL

Work following rows with A.

Row 1 (WS): P12 (15), p2tog, p1, turn.

Row 2: Sl 1, k5 (7), ssk, k1, turn.

Row 3: Sl 1, p6 (8), p2tog, p1, turn.

Row 4: Sl 1, k7 (9), ssk, k1, turn.

Row 5: Sl 1, p8 (10), p2tog, p1, turn.

Row 6: Sl 1, k9 (11), ssk, k1, turn.

Row 7: Sl 1, p10 (12), p2tog, p1, turn.

Row 8: Sl 1, k11 (13), ssk, turn.

Row 9: Sl 1, p12 (14), p2tog, turn—13 (15) sts.

INSTEP

Redistribute stitches as follows: With RS of heel facing and A, knit the first 7 (8) sts of the heel onto a spare needle and hold away from work. Continuing on the heel sts for needle #3, knit the remaining 6 (7) sts and pick up and knit 12 (13) sts along left side of heel flap—18 (20) sts on needle #3. For needle #1, work

in established cable pattern across the instep sts—22 (24) sts on needle #1. For needle #2, pick up and knit 11 (12) sts along right side of heel flap, then knit 7 (8) heel sts on spare needle—18 (20) sts on needle #2.

Round 1: Join A in middle of heel between needles #2 and 3, and work as follows:

Needle #3: Knit;

Needle #1: Work in established cable pattern;

Needle #2: Knit.

Round 2:

Needle #3: Knit to last 3 sts, ssk, k1;

Needle #1: Work in established cable pattern;

Needle #2: K1, k2tog, knit to end.

Repeat rounds 1 and 2 until needles #2 and #3 each have 11 (12) sts remaining.

Work rounds in established pattern, without further decreasing, until the foot, measured from the heel, measures 5½ (7)"/14 (18)cm. Discontinue cable pattern on needle #1.

SHAPE TOE

Change to B.

Round 1:

Needle #1: K1, k2tog, knit to last 3 sts, ssk, k1;

Needle #2: K1, k2tog, knit to end;

Needle #3: Knit to last 3 sts, ssk, k1.

Round 2: Knit.

Repeat last 2 rounds in the following color sequence: 2 rounds with D, 2 rounds with C. With A, repeat last 2 rounds until 8 sts remain on needle #1, and 4 sts remain on needles #2 and #3. Slip sts from needle #3 onto needle #2, so there are two needles with 8 sts on each. Cut yarn, leaving a 30"/76cm tail to weave toe sts together.

FINISHING

Sew small opening at top of cuff. Tie off and weave in all ends (except long tail for finishing toe).

KITCHENER STITCH TO FINISH TOE

Thread long tail onto tapestry needle.

Step 1: With WS together, hold both knitting needles together and even, insert tapestry needle into first st on front needle as if to purl and draw yarn through. Leave st on needle.

Step 2: Hold yarn in back, insert tapestry needle as if to knit into first st on back needle, and draw yarn through. Leave st on needle.

Step 3: Hold yarn in front, insert tapestry needle as if to knit through first st on front needle, and draw yarn through. Slip st off needle. Insert tapestry needle through next st on front needle as if to purl and draw yarn through. Leave st on needle.

Step 4: Insert tapestry needle as if to purl through first st on back needle and draw yarn through. Slip st off needle. Insert tapestry needle through next st on back needle as if to knit and draw yarn through. Leave st on needle.

Repeat steps 3 and 4 until all but 1 st has been eliminated. Draw yarn through this st to secure.

Designer Tip

When working with dpn, as you move from one needle to the next, cross the tip of the new needle over the tip of the needle just worked. Hold the yarn firmly when working the first st on the new needle. This will avoid "holes" in the finished piece.

This project was knit with:

Sassy Skein's Key West Karibbean Kotton, DK weight, 100% mercerized cotton, 1.75oz/50g = approx 105yd/95m per ball

(A) 1 ball, color #127
(B) 1 ball, color #128
(C) 1 ball, color #111
(D) 1 ball, color #110

Cable Guy Scarf

SKILL LEVEL

Intermediate

SIZES

Small (Large)

FINISHED MEASUREMENTS

Length 46 (58)"/117 (147)cm,
excluding fringe
Width 4"/10cm

MATERIALS AND TOOLS

Approx total: 370 (592)yd/333 (533)m of
(4) Aran weight yarn, cotton
Color A: 74yd/67m of (4) Aran weight
yarn, cotton, in brown
Color B: 148 (222)yd/133 (200)m of (4)
Aran weight yarn, cotton, in green

Girls go crazy for a

Color C: 74 (148)yd/67 (133)m of (4) Aran
weight yarn, cotton, in dark yellow
Color D: 74 (148)yd/67 (133)m of (4) Aran
weight yarn, cotton, in orange
Knitting needles: 5mm (size 8 U.S.) *or size
to obtain gauge*
Cable needle
Crochet hook
Tapestry needle

GAUGE

26 sts and 24 rows = 4"/10cm in
Lattice Stitch
Always take time to check your gauge.

SPECIAL ABBREVIATIONS

Cable 4 sts back (C4B): Slip 2 sts onto
cable needle and hold in back, k2, k2
from cable needle.
Cable 4 sts front (C4F): Slip 2 sts onto
cable needle and hold in front, k2 sts,
k2 from cable needle.

LATTICE STITCH

Rows 1, 3, 5, and 7 (WS): Purl.

Row 2 (RS): Knit.

Row 4: K1, *C4B, k4, C4F; repeat from * to last st, k1.

Row 6: Knit.

Row 8: K3, C4F, C4B, *k4, C4F, C4B; repeat from * to last 3 sts, k3.

Repeat rows 1–8 for pattern.

sharp-dressed guy.

Scarf

With A, cast on 26 sts.

Work 4 rows in Garter Stitch (knit every row).

With D, work 8-row Lattice Stitch pattern 3 (5) times.

With C, work 8-row Lattice Stitch pattern 3 (5) times.

With B, work 8-row Lattice Stitch pattern 23 (25) times.

With C, work 8-row Lattice Stitch pattern 3 (5) times.

With D, work 8-row Lattice Stitch pattern 3 (5) times.

Next row (WS): With D, purl.

With A, work 4 rows in Garter Stitch. Bind off.

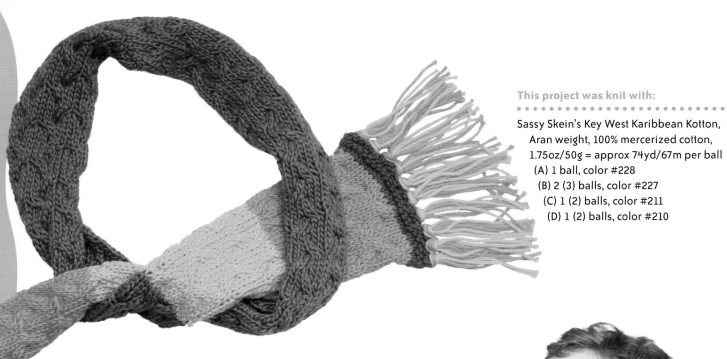

This project was knit with:

Sassy Skein's Key West Karibbean Kotton,
Aran weight, 100% mercerized cotton,
1.75oz/50g = approx 74yd/67m per ball
(A) 1 ball, color #228
(B) 2 (3) balls, color #227
(C) 1 (2) balls, color #211
(D) 1 (2) balls, color #210

FINISHING

FRINGE

Make 10 tassels on each end. Cut 8"/20cm lengths of C and D. Fold four strands (two of each color) in half for each tassel, forming a loop. Using a crochet hook, draw the tassel loop through a secure place at the end of the scarf. Draw the ends of the fringe through the loop and pull tightly. After all of your tassels are in place, trim the ends of your fringe evenly to desired length.

Weave in ends on wrong side of scarf.

Note: See page 17 for more information on making fringe.

Leader of the Pack Sack

SKILL LEVEL

Easy

FINISHED MEASUREMENTS

Sack 9"/23cm wide x 10"/25cm deep x
15"/38cm high
Handles 30"/76cm

MATERIALS AND TOOLS

Approx total: 270yd/246m of (6) bulky
weight yarn, alpaca/wool
Color A: 225yd/203m of (6) bulky weight
yarn, alpaca/wool, in orange
Color B: 45yd/41m of (6) bulky weight
yarn, alpaca/wool, in green

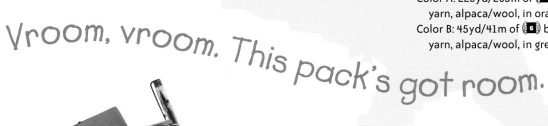

Vroom, vroom. This pack's got room.

Knitting needle: 10mm (size 15 U.S.)
24"/61cm circular needle or size to
obtain gauge
10mm (size 15 U.S.) set of 2 double-
pointed needles for I-cord
Tapestry needle
Crochet hook
Stitch marker
1 decorative button

GAUGE

10 sts and 12 rows = 4"/10cm in
Stockinette Stitch (knit every round)
Always take time to check your gauge.

PATTERN STITCH

SEED STITCH
Over an odd number of sts.
Row 1 (RS): *K1, p1; repeat from *, end k1.
Repeat row 1 for pattern.

Backpack

BOTTOM

With A, cast on 23 sts.

Work back and forth on circular needle in Seed Stitch until bottom measures 10"/25cm from beginning.

BODY

Next Round: Pivot piece to work along side of bottom, pick up and knit 20 sts along side; pick up and knit 23 sts along the cast-on edge; pick up and knit 20 sts along the remaining side—86 sts (including 23 sts originally on needle). Place a marker to indicate the beginning of the round. Join to work sts in the round.

Work in Stockinette Stitch until body measures 13"/33cm. Change to B.

Next 2 rounds: Knit.

Next round (drawstring round): *K2tog, yo; repeat from * around.

Next round: Knit.

Bind off.

FRONT POCKET

With B, cast on 17 sts.

Work back and forth on circular needle in Seed Stitch until piece measures 6"/15cm from beginning. Bind off.

POCKET FLAP

With B, cast on 17 sts.

Rows 1 (RS) and 2: Work 2 rows, back and forth on circular needle in Seed Stitch.

Rows 3–8: Work in Stockinette Stitch, decrease 1 st at each edge—5 sts rem.

Row 9 (RS, buttonhole row): Decrease 1 st, yo, k1, decrease 1 st—4 sts.

Row 10: Decrease 2 sts—2 sts.

Row 11: Decrease 1 st. Fasten off st.

HANDLE

With B and 2 double-pointed needles, cast on 4 sts. Make an I-cord, 30"/102cm long.

FINISHING

Place front pocket on sack, approximately 1"/3cm from lower edge and centered on front of sack. With B, sew sides and lower edge of pocket to front of sack. With B, sew pocket flap above top of pocket. Sew flower button to top of pocket aligned with buttonhole.

Sew one end of the handle to the lower right-hand corner of the back of the sack. Weave the other end of the handle through one of the drawstring openings, skip 5 to 6 openings, and weave the handle back through to the right side of the sack. Sew the other end of the handle to the opposite lower corner of the back of the sack.

DRAWSTRING

With A, single crochet a chain 48"/122cm long. Weave the drawstring through the drawstring opening at the top edge of the sack, taking care to center the drawstring so it ties at the front of the bag.

DRAWSTRING TASSEL

Cut four 7"/18cm lengths of A. Pull the strands through the last chain of the drawstring and fold the strands in half. Using the end of one strand, wrap it around the tassel several times and knot securely. Trim strands evenly. Repeat on other end of drawstring.

Note: See page 17 for more information on making tassels.

Note: See page 104 for information on making I-cord. As an alternative to knitted I-cord, you can make I-cord with a spool knitter.

Note: See page 106 for information about picking up stitches.

This project was knit with:
. . . .

Blue Sky Alpaca's Bulky Hand Dyes, bulky weight, 50% alpaca/50% wool, 3.5oz/100g = approx 45yd/41m per ball

(A) 5 balls, color #1015

(B) 1 ball, color #1017

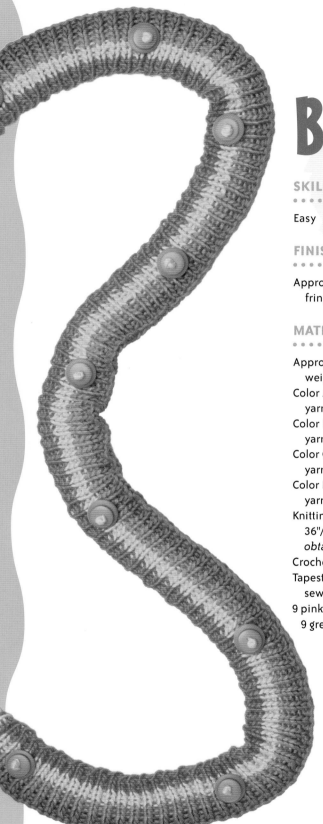

Button Belt

FINISHED MEASUREMENTS

· ·

Approx 44 x 1½"/112 x 4cm, excluding fringe

MATERIALS AND TOOLS

· ·

Approx total: 296yd/266m of (**4**) Aran weight yarn, cotton

Color A: 74yd/67m of (**4**) Aran weight yarn, cotton, in pink

Color B: 74yd/67m of (**4**) Aran weight yarn, cotton, in yellow

Color C: 74yd/67m of (**4**) Aran weight yarn, cotton, in orange

Color D: 74yd/67m of (**4**) Aran weight yarn, cotton, in green

Knitting needle: 4mm (size 6 U.S.) 24–36"/61–91cm circular needle *or size to obtain gauge*

Crochet hook

Tapestry needle (with a small eye) for sewing buttons

9 pink buttons, ⅝"/16mm

9 green buttons, ⅞"/22mm

GAUGE

· ·

22 sts and 28 rows = 4"/10cm in K1, P1 Rib
Always take time to check your gauge.

PATTERN STITCH

· ·

K1, P1 RIB

Row 1: *K1, p1; repeat from * to end.

Repeat row 1 for pattern.

A button a day

Belt

Note: Work back and forth on circular needle, not in the round.

With A, cast on 242 sts.

With A, work 2 rows in K1, P1 Rib.

With B, work 3 rows in K1, P1 Rib.

With C, work 3 rows in K1, P1 Rib.

With D, work 2 rows in K1, P1 Rib, then bind off in Rib.

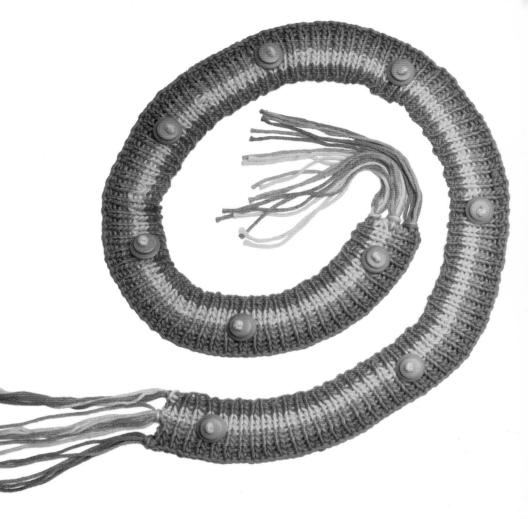

FINISHING

FRINGE

Make three tassels on each end. Cut 14"/36cm lengths of yarn, in coordinating colors. Fold three strands of yarn in half for each tassel, forming a loop. Using a crochet hook, draw the tassel loop through a secure place at the end of the belt. Draw the ends of the fringe through the loop and pull tightly. Include the tail of yarn from your cast on, color changes, and bind off with the appropriate tassels. After all of your tassels are in place, trim the ends of your fringe evenly to desired length.

keeps the doctor away.

BUTTON DETAIL

Stack small buttons on top of large buttons. Center buttons evenly spaced along length of belt. Using a long strand of B, sew the buttons in place with French Knots. One long strand can be used to sew all of the buttons; weave the strand evenly along the wrong side of the belt between buttons, taking care not to pull the strand too tightly.

Weave in ends on wrong side of belt.

Note: See page 17 for more information on making fringe.

This project was knit with:

Sassy Skein's Key West Karibbean Kotton, Aran weight, 100% mercerized cotton, 1.75oz/50g = approx 74yd/67m per ball
(A) 1 ball, color #206
(B) 1 ball, color #211
(C) 1 ball, color #215
(D) 1 ball, color #204

Perfect Pillows

SKILL LEVEL

Easy

FINISHED MEASUREMENTS

13 x 13"/33 x 33cm

MATERIALS AND TOOLS

Approx total: 518yd/466m of (**4**) Aran weight yarn, cotton

Color A: 148yd/133m of (**4**) Aran weight yarn, cotton, in blue

Color B: 148yd/133m of (**4**) Aran weight yarn, cotton, in white

Color C: 74yd/67m of (**4**) Aran weight yarn, cotton, in yellow

Color D: 74yd/67m of (**4**) Aran weight yarn, cotton, in red

Color E: 74yd/67m of (**4**) Aran weight yarn, cotton, in orange

Knitting needles: 5mm (size 8 U.S.) *or size to obtain gauge*

Tapestry needle

4 small red buttons (for each pillow)

Polyester fiberfill (washable)

Crochet hook

GAUGE

18 sts and 24 rows = 4"/10cm in Stockinette Stitch (knit on RS, purl on WS)

Always take time to check your gauge.

Make sure you have plenty for a pillow fight!

Pillow

FRONT PANEL

With A, cast on 60 sts.

Work Stockinette Stitch in the following color sequence: *8 rows with A, 8 rows with B; repeat from * 3 more times, 8 rows with A.

With A, continue in Stockinette Stitch until piece measures 13"/33cm.

Bind off.

BACK PANEL

Work as for front panel.

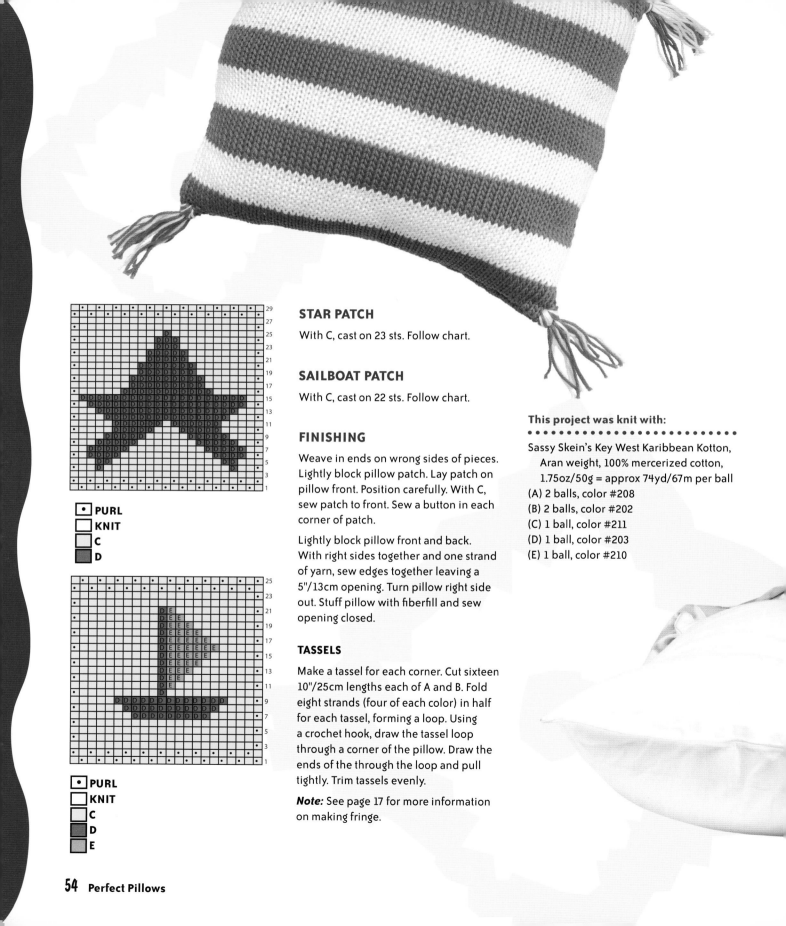

STAR PATCH

With C, cast on 23 sts. Follow chart.

SAILBOAT PATCH

With C, cast on 22 sts. Follow chart.

FINISHING

Weave in ends on wrong sides of pieces. Lightly block pillow patch. Lay patch on pillow front. Position carefully. With C, sew patch to front. Sew a button in each corner of patch.

Lightly block pillow front and back. With right sides together and one strand of yarn, sew edges together leaving a 5"/13cm opening. Turn pillow right side out. Stuff pillow with fiberfill and sew opening closed.

TASSELS

Make a tassel for each corner. Cut sixteen 10"/25cm lengths each of A and B. Fold eight strands (four of each color) in half for each tassel, forming a loop. Using a crochet hook, draw the tassel loop through a corner of the pillow. Draw the ends of the through the loop and pull tightly. Trim tassels evenly.

Note: See page 17 for more information on making fringe.

This project was knit with:

Sassy Skein's Key West Karibbean Kotton, Aran weight, 100% mercerized cotton, 1.75oz/50g = approx 74yd/67m per ball

(A) 2 balls, color #208
(B) 2 balls, color #202
(C) 1 ball, color #211
(D) 1 ball, color #203
(E) 1 ball, color #210

• PURL
☐ KNIT
☐ C
☐ D

• PURL
☐ KNIT
☐ C
☐ D
☐ E

Go Team

SKILL LEVEL

Easy/Intermediate

SIZES

Small (Large)

FINISHED MEASUREMENTS

Circumference 16 (19)"/41 (48)cm
Height 8½ (10)"/22 (25)cm

My team wins when I wear this lucky hat.

MATERIALS AND TOOLS

Approx total: 400yd/360m of  worsted
   weight yarn, acrylic/wool in your
   favorite team's colors
Color A: 200yd/180m of 4 worsted
   weight yarn, acrylic/wool, in orange
Color B: 200yd/180m of 4 worsted
   weight yarn, acrylic/wool, in white
Knitting needles: 4.5mm (size 7 U.S.)
   10–12"/25–31cm circular needle and
   set of 4 double-pointed needles *or size
   to obtain gauge*
Tapestry needle

GAUGE

20 sts and 28 rows = 4"/10cm in
Stockinette Stitch (knit every round)
Always take time to check your gauge.

PATTERN STITCH

K2, P2 RIB

Row 1: *K2, p2; repeat from * to end.

Repeat row 1 for pattern.

Hat

With A and circular needle, cast on 88
(104) sts. Lay sts down on a flat surface
to be sure that the cast-on sts are not
twisted. Place a marker to indicate the
beginning of the round. Join to work sts in
the round.

TURNED-UP BRIM

Work in K2, P2 Rib until piece measures 4
(5)"/10 (13)cm from beginning.

BODY

Round 1: With B, knit.

Round 2: With A, knit.

Rounds 3–5: With B, knit.

Rounds 6–8: With A, knit.

Rounds 9 and 10: *K2 with A, k2 with B;
repeat from * around.

Rounds 11 and 12: *K2 with B, k2 with A;
repeat from * around.

Rounds 13–15: With A, knit.

Rounds 16–18: With B, knit.

Round 19: With A, knit.

Round 20: With A, purl.

Round 21: With A, *k1, p1; repeat from *
around.

Round 22: With B, *p1, k1; repeat from *
around.

Repeat 21st and 22nd rounds 4 (6) more
times.

Last 3 Rounds: With A, knit.

CROWN

Round 1: With B, *k11 (13), place marker;
repeat from * 7 more times.

Round 2: *Knit to within 2 sts of marker,
k2tog; repeat from * 8 more times, knit
around—80 (96) sts.

Repeat round 2 until 16 sts remain.
Cut yarn leaving a long tail. Thread tail
through remaining 6 sts, pull tight, and tie
off. Weave in yarn tail on WS of hat.

FINISHING

POM-POM

Using both yarn colors, make a pom-pom
as described on page 17. Secure pom-pom
to top of hat.

This project was knit with:

Plymouth Yarn's Encore, worsted weight,
75% acrylic/25% washable wool, 3.5oz/
100g = approx 200yd/180m per ball
(A) 1 ball, color #1383
(B) 1 ball, color #0208

Listen Up! MP3 (or Cell) Case

SKILL LEVEL

Beginner

SIZES

Colorway #1 (Colorway #2)

FINISHED MEASUREMENTS

Case 4½ (5)"/11 (13)cm tall x 3 (4)"/8 (10)cm wide
Handle 30"/76cm long
Button Flap 3"/8cm long

MATERIALS AND TOOLS

Approx total: 164yd/148m of 〔4〕 Aran weight yarn, cotton (makes 2 projects)

COLORWAY #1:

Color A: 82yd/74m of 〔4〕 Aran weight yarn, cotton, in olive green

COLORWAY #2:

Color B: 82yd/74m of 〔4〕 Aran weight yarn, cotton, in aqua blue
Knitting needle: 4.5mm (size 7 U.S.) *or size to obtain gauge*
Tapestry needle
1 coordinating button, ½–¾"/13–19mm diameter
1 brown bead, ½"/13mm diameter (for colorway #1)
1 metal clip (for colorway #1)
7 coordinating beads, ½"/13mm diameter (for colorway #2)

GAUGE

22 sts and 28 rows = 4"/10cm in Garter
Stitch (knit every row)
Always take time to check your gauge.

Got tunes? Take 'em wherever you go.

Bag

With desired colorway, cast on 45 (50) sts.

Work in Garter Stitch until piece
measures 4½ (5)"/11 (13)cm.

Next row (start button flap): Bind off
first 4 sts, continue in Garter Stitch to
end—41 (46) sts.

Next row: Bind off 29 (34) sts, continue in
Garter Stitch over last 12 sts.

Next row: K2tog, knit to last 2 sts, k2tog—
10 sts.

Repeat last row until there are 4 sts
remaining.

Work even in Garter Stitch over these 4
sts until button flap measures 2¾"/7cm.

Next row (buttonhole): K1, k2tog, yo, k1.

Last row: Knit.

Bind off.

FINISHING

Fold bag in half, with right sides facing
out. With matching yarn and tapestry
needle, sew lower edge and side seam.
Weave in ends on wrong side of bag.
Gently block bag. Sew button in place.

TASSEL (FOR COLORWAY #1)

Cut seven strands of A, 10"/25cm long.
Draw strands through the ring on the
metal clip and around the base of the
button flap. Fold strands in half and tie an
overhand knot. Thread bead onto ends
of strands. Wrap one strand around tassel
just below bead and tie securely. Trim
tassel evenly.

STRAP (FOR COLORWAY #2)

Cut four 9yd/8m lengths of B. Fold yarn
and pull through several stitches at top
edge of bag on one side. Make a strap by
following the Braided Strap instructions
on page 19.

Repeat the three steps, placing a bead
after the first six knots and then every 20
knots; after the last bead, braid six final
knots to the end of the handle. Sew the
handle to other side of case, creating a
tassle with strands of yarn from handle.

This project was knit with:

Cascade Yarn's Luna, Aran weight, 100%
Peruvian cotton, 1.75oz/50g = approx
82yd/74m per ball
(A) 1 ball, color #716
(B) 1 ball, color #714

Funky Fanny Pack

A handy pack for kids on the go...

SKILL LEVEL

Intermediate

FINISHED MEASUREMENTS

Bag 7½ x 5½"/19 x 14cm
Waist strap 28"/71cm, or as desired

MATERIALS AND TOOLS

Approx total: 296yd/266m of  Aran
  weight yarn, cotton
Color A: 74yd/67m of Aran weight
  yarn, cotton, in green
Color B: 74yd/67m of Aran weight
  yarn, cotton, in aqua

Color C: 74yd/67m of Aran weight
  yarn, cotton, in red
Color D: 74yd/67m of Aran weight
  yarn, cotton, in yellow
Knitting needles: 5mm (size 8 U.S.) *or size
  to obtain gauge*
Tapestry needle
  2 D-rings, 1¼–1½"/32–38mm
    7"/18cm red jumbo zipper
    Sewing needle and red
      sewing thread

GAUGE

16 sts and 20 rows =
4"/10cm in Garter Stitch
(knit every row)
*Always take time to
check your gauge.*

Fanny Pack

FRONT

With two strands of A held together, cast on 20 sts.

Work in Garter Stitch until piece measures 9"/23cm from beginning.

Bind off.

BACK

With two strands of B held together, work as for Front.

SIDES

With two strands of D held together, cast on 6 sts.

Work in Garter Stitch until piece measures 19"/48cm from beginning.

Bind off.

WAIST STRAP (MAKE 2)

Note: Strap is knit in two pieces.

With two strands of C held together, cast on 6 sts.

Work in Garter Stitch until piece measures desired length (one piece should be 10"/25cm, the other 23"/58cm).

Bind off.

FINISHING

Lightly block the pieces if needed. Lay front and side pieces together so that one long edge of side wraps around two short edges and lower edge of front. Working from the wrong side with one strand of matching yarn and tapestry needle, sew the two pieces together along long edge of side, beginning at top side edge and working around front piece, ending at top edge of the opposite end of front piece.

Slide two D-rings over short waist strap. Fold short waist strap in half with D-rings at fold. With tapestry needle and matching yarn, sew side edges of short waist strap together leaving ½"/1cm open at fold for D-rings.

Lay back and side pieces together so that the unsewn long edge of side wraps around two short edges and lower edge of back. Insert ends of waist strap pieces, one on each side, between the back and side pieces 1"/3cm below top edge. Working from wrong side with one strand of matching yarn and tapestry needle, sew the pieces together along long edge of side, beginning at top side edge and working around back piece, ending at top edge of the opposite end of back piece.

ZIPPER

Lay zipper in place at top of bag. Working from wrong side with sewing needle and red sewing thread, sew the zipper in place securely, allowing the teeth and some of the red zipper tape to show.

Weave in ends on wrong side of fanny pack. Turn fanny pack right side out and lightly block again if desired.

ZIPPER TASSEL

Cut two 8"/20cm lengths of each color, for a total of eight strands. Pull the strands through the hole in the zipper tab, and fold the strands in half. Using the end of one strand, wrap it around the tassel several times and knot securely. Trim strands evenly.

Note: This project is worked double stranded. Hold two strands of yarn together throughout.

This project was knit with:
• •

Sassy Skein's Key West Karibbean Kotton, Aran weight, 100% mercerized cotton, 1.75oz/50g = approx 74yd/67m per ball
(A) 1 ball, color #204
(B) 1 ball, color #208
(C) 1 ball, color #203
(D) 1 ball, color #211

EZ Leg Warmers

Perfect for warming up and staying cool.

SKILL LEVEL

Easy

SIZES

Small (Large)

FINISHED MEASUREMENTS

Circumference 9½ (11)"/24 (28)cm
Length 12 (14)"/31 (36)cm

MATERIALS AND TOOLS

Approx total: 490 (686)yd/441 (617)m
    of (4) Aran weight yarn, cotton/
    polyester
Color A: 98 (196)yd/88 (176)m of (4)
    Aran weight yarn, cotton/polyester,
    in lime green
Color B: 196 (196)yd/176 (176)m of (4)
    Aran weight yarn, cotton/polyester,
    in light orange
Color C: 196 (294)yd/176 (265)m of (4)
    Aran weight yarn, cotton/polyester,
    in dark orange
Knitting needles: 6mm (size 10 U.S.) *or
    size to obtain gauge*
Crochet hook for fringe (optional)
Tapestry needle

GAUGE

19 sts and 28 rows = 4"/10cm in Wide Rib

Always take time to check your gauge.

PATTERN STITCH

WIDE RIB

Row 1 (RS): *K3, p1; repeat from * to end.

Row 2 (WS): Purl.

Repeat rows 1 and 2 for pattern.

Leg Warmers

LOWER CUFF

With A, cast on 44 (52) sts, leaving a long tail to sew back seam.

Row 1 (WS): Knit.

Work 5 rows in Wide Rib pattern.

Row 7: Knit.

LEG

Work Wide Rib pattern in the following color sequence: 12 (14) rows with C, *6 rows with B, 2 rows with A, 1 row with B, 1 row with C, 2 rows with A, 4 (6) rows with B, 12 (14) rows with C; repeat from * once more, 4 (6) rows with B.

Next row (RS): With B, purl.

TOP FOLD-OVER CUFF

Row 1 (WS): P1, k3, *p1, k3; repeat from * to end.

Row 2 (RS): Purl.

Repeat rows 1 and 2 in the following color sequence: 6 rows with B, 7 (9) rows with C, 2 rows with A, 2 rows with C, 5 (7) rows with A, 1 row with B.

Next row: With B, purl.

Bind off as if to knit.

FINISHING

With yarn tail, sew back center seam, from lower edge to top edge, leaving 1½"/4cm open at top of fold-over cuff.

FRINGE (OPTIONAL)

Cut 6"/15cm lengths of all three colors. Fold three strands (one of each color) in half for each tassel, forming a loop. Using a crochet hook, draw the tassel loop through a secure place at the top edge of the fold-over cuff. Draw the ends of the fringe through the loop and pull tightly. Work number of fringe desired, evenly spaced all the way around the tops of both leg warmers. After all of your tassels are in place, trim the ends of the fringe evenly.

Weave in ends on wrong sides of leg warmers.

Note: EZ Leg Warmers are not worked in the round. However, you may work back and forth on a circular needle, or use straight needles.

Note: See page 17 for more information on making fringe.

This project was knit with:
. . . .

Skacel's Schulana Supercotton, Aran
  weight, 70% cotton/30% polyester,
  1.75oz/50g = approx 98yd/88m per ball
(A) 1 (2) balls, color #65
(B) 2 balls, color #72
(C) 2 (3) balls, color #56

Pick Pocket for Boys

Hmmm...that pocket

SKILL LEVEL

Intermediate

SIZES

Small (Large)

FINISHED MEASUREMENTS

Width 4½"/11cm
Length 56 (62)"/142 (157)cm

MATERIALS AND TOOLS

Approx total: 450 (600)yd/405 (540)m of
🔵 worsted weight yarn, cotton
Color A: 150 (150)yd/135 (135)m of 🔵
worsted weight yarn, cotton, in blue

Color B: 150 (300)yd/135 (270)m of
🔵 worsted weight yarn, cotton, in
off-white
Color C: 150 (150)yd/135 (135)m of 🔵
worsted weight yarn, cotton, in aqua
Knitting needles: 4.5mm (size 7 U.S.) *or
size to obtain gauge*
Tapestry needle

GAUGE

28 sts and 22 rows = 4"/10cm in Twisted
Rib Stitch
Always take time to check your gauge.

SPECIAL ABBREVIATIONS

Right Twist (RT): K2tog leaving both sts
on needle; insert right-hand needle
between the 2 sts just knit and knit the
first st again; slide both sts from left-
hand needle.

Knit one through back loop (k1 tbl):
Knit stitch through back loop (rather
than front loop as usual).

PATTERN STITCH

TWISTED RIB STITCH

Row 1 (RS): K1, *k1 tbl, p1; repeat from *
to last 2 sts, k1 tbl, k1.

Row 2 (WS): P1, *p1, k1; repeat from * to
last 2 sts, p2.

Repeat rows 1 and 2 for pattern.

Scarf

POCKET EDGING

With A, cast on 30 sts.

Rows 1–6: Garter St (knit every row).

POCKET

Row 1 (WS): P2, *k2, p2; repeat from * to end.

Row 2: K2, *p2, k2; repeat from * to end.

Row 3: Repeat row 1

Row 4: K2, p2, *RT, p2; repeat from * to last 2 sts, k2.

Repeat rows 1–4 until 11 (12) twists have been worked. End with row 4.

Work 3 rows in Garter Stitch (knit every row).

Next row: Knit, increase 1 st—31 sts.

BODY

Note: Pocket ended on a right side row. Turn work so that the wrong side of pocket is facing you. The wrong side of the pocket now becomes the right side of the scarf.

With B, work Twisted Rib Stitch for 11 (12)"/28 (31)cm. End with a RS (scarf) row.

Continue Twisted Rib Stitch in the following color sequence: *2 rows with A, 2 rows with C, 2 rows with B; repeat from * 3 (4) more times, 10 (12) rows with B, 4 rows with A, 4 rows with B, 4 rows with C, 4 rows with B, 4 rows with A, 21 (22) rows with B, 2 rows with A, 6 rows with C, 2 rows with A, 21 (22) rows with B, 4 rows with A, 4 rows with B, 4 rows with C, 4 rows with B, 4 rows with A, 12 (14) rows with B, **2 rows with C, 2 rows with A, 2 rows with B; repeat from ** 3 (4) more times.

With B, continue Twisted Rib Stitch for 11 (12)"/28 (31)cm. End on a RS row.

Work 3 rows in Garter Stitch.

Next row (RS): Knit, decrease 1 st—30 sts.

POCKET

Note: Body ended on a right side row. Turn work so that the wrong side of the scarf is facing you. The wrong side of the scarf now becomes the right side of the pocket.

With C
Row 1: K2, p2, *RT, p2; repeat from * to last 2 sts, k2.

Row 2 (WS): P2, *k2, p2; repeat from * to end.

Row 3: K2, *p2, k2; repeat from * to end.

Row 4: Repeat row 2.

Repeat rows 1–4 until 11 (12) twists have been worked. End with row 4.

POCKET EDGING

Work 6 rows in Garter Stitch.

Bind off as if to purl.

FINISHING

From the right side of the scarf, fold each pocket up so that right side of pocket is now showing, to a point slightly above the Garter Stitch rows. Secure with pins or clips to keep pocket straight. Sew side seams together.

Weave in ends carefully so that both sides of the scarf are clean and smooth.

This project was knit with:

● ●

Blue Sky Alpaca's Cotton, worsted weight, 100% cotton, 3.5oz/100g = approx 150yd/135m per ball

(A) 1 ball, color #632

(B) 1 (2) balls, color #614

(C) 1 ball, color #630

Pick Pocket for Girls

SKILL LEVEL

Intermediate

SIZES

Small (Large)

FINISHED MEASUREMENTS

Width 4½"/11cm
Length 56 (62)"/142 (157)cm

Keep your lip balm handy.

MATERIALS AND TOOLS

Approx total: 600yd/540m of (4) worsted
  weight yarn, cotton
Color A: 300yd/270m of (4) worsted
  weight yarn, cotton, in hot pink
Color B: 300yd/270m of (4) worsted
  weight yarn, cotton, in white
Knitting needles: 4.5mm (size 7 U.S.) *or
  size to obtain gauge*
Tapestry needle
2 buttons, 1¼"/32mm diameter
Crochet hook for pocket Lizzie loops
  (optional)

GAUGE

28 sts and 22 rows = 4"/10cm in Twisted
  Rib Stitch
Always take time to check your gauge.

SPECIAL ABBREVIATIONS

Right Twist (RT): K2tog leaving both sts
  on needle; insert right-hand needle
  between the 2 sts just knit and knit the
  first st again; slide both sts from left-
  hand needle.
Knit one through back loop (k1 tbl):
  Knit stitch through back loop (rather
  than front loop as usual).

PATTERN STITCH

TWISTED RIB STITCH

Row 1 (RS): K1, *k1 tbl, p1; repeat from * to last 2 sts, k1 tbl, k1.

Row 2 (WS): P1, *p1, k1; repeat from * to last 2 sts, p2.

Repeat rows 1 and 2 for pattern.

Scarf

PICOT EDGING

With B, cast on 30 sts.

Row 1 (WS): Purl.

Row 2 (RS): Knit.

Row 3: Purl.

Row 4: K1, *k2tog, yo; repeat from * to last st, k1.

Row 5: Purl.

Row 6: Knit.

POCKET

Row 1: P2, *k2, p2; repeat from * to end.

Row 2: K2, *p2, k2; repeat from * to end.

Row 3: Repeat row 1.

Row 4: K2, p2, *RT, p2; repeat from * to last 2 sts, k2.

Repeat rows 1–4 until 11 (12) twists have been worked. End with row 4.

Work 3 rows in Garter Stitch (knit every row).

Next row: Knit, increase 1 st—31 sts.

BODY

Note: Pocket ended on a right side row. Turn work so that the wrong side of pocket is facing you. The wrong side of the pocket now becomes the right side of the scarf.

With A, work Twisted Rib Stitch for 11 (12)"/28 (31)cm. End with a RS (scarf) row.

Continue Twisted Rib Stitch in the following color sequence: *2 rows with B, 2 rows with A; repeat from * 4 (5) more times, 2 rows with B, 12 (14) rows with A, 4 rows with B, 4 rows with A, 4 rows with B, 4 rows with A, 4 rows with B, 21 (24) rows with A, 21 (24) rows with B, 4 rows with A, 4 rows with B, 4 rows with A, 4 rows with B, 4 rows with A, 12 (14) rows with B, **2 rows with A, 2 rows with B; repeat from ** 4 (5) more times, 2 rows with A.

With B, continue Twisted Rib Stitch for 11 (12)"/28 (31)cm. End on a RS row.

Work 3 rows in Garter Stitch.

Next row (RS): Knit, decrease 1 st—30 sts.

POCKET

Note: Body ended on a right side row. Turn work so that the wrong side of scarf is facing you. The wrong side of the scarf now becomes the right side of the pocket.

With A

Row 1: K2, p2, *RT, p2; repeat from * to last 2 sts, k2.

Row 2 (WS): P2, *k2, p2; repeat from * to end.

Row 3: K2, *p2, k2; repeat from * to end.

Row 4: Repeat row 2.

Repeat rows 1–4 until 11 (12) twists have been worked. End with row 4.

PICOT EDGING

Work 3 rows in Stockinette Stitch.

Next row (WS): P1, *p2tog, yo; repeat from * to last st, p1.

Next row: Knit.

Next row: Purl.

Bind off.

FINISHING

At the picot edging row, fold the top of each pocket to the wrong side of the pocket and sew down. From the right side of the scarf fold each pocket up, so that right side of pocket is now showing, to a point slightly above the Garter Stitch rows. Secure with pins or clips to keep pocket straight. Sew side seams together.

Decoration on the pocket is optional. The scarf, as shown, has a large button on the face of the pocket that is kept closed with an 8"/20cm crocheted chain loop attached to the back inside of the pocket. Lizzie loops are worked along the top of each pocket.

Weave in ends carefully so that both sides of the scarf are clean and smooth.

Note: See page 18 for more information on making Lizzie loops.

This project was knit with:

• •

Blue Sky Alpaca's Cotton, worsted weight, 100% cotton, 3.5oz/100g = approx 150yd/135m per ball
(A) 2 balls, color #627
(B) 2 balls, color #615

Strings and Stripes Scarf

These silly strings tickle my funny bone.

SKILL LEVEL

Easy

SIZES

Small (Large)

FINISHED MEASUREMENTS

48 (56) x 2½"/122 (142) x 6cm, including pom-poms

MATERIALS AND TOOLS

Approx total: 666yd/600m of Aran weight yarn, cotton

Color A: 222yd/200m of Aran weight yarn, cotton, in ecru

Color B: 222yd/200m of Aran weight yarn, cotton, in dark blue

Color C: 222yd/200m of Aran weight yarn, cotton, in red

Knitting needle: 6mm (size 10 U.S.) 36"/91cm circular needle *or size to obtain gauge*

Tapestry needle

GAUGE

10 sts and 18 rows = 4"/10cm in Stockinette Stitch (knit on RS, purl on WS)

Always take time to check your gauge.

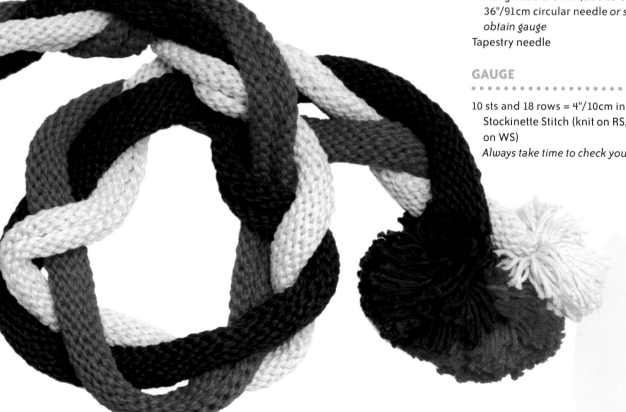

And all my other bones, too!

Scarf Section (make 3)

Note: Work back and forth on circular needle, not in the round.

With two strands of A held together, cast on 120 (140) sts.

Row 1: Purl.

Work 9 rows in Stockinette Stitch.

Bind off as if to purl.

Repeat these instructions with B and then with C.

Stretch each section gently from each end to allow edges to curl inward.

FINISHING

Weave in ends on knit sides of scarf sections.

POM-POMS

Make two pom-poms with each color as described on page 17. Secure one pom-pom to each end of matching colored section.

Braid the three sections loosely. With tapestry needle, sew through the ends of all three sections, approximately 2"/5cm above the pom-poms, to secure ends.

Note: This project is worked double stranded. Hold two strands of yarn together throughout. The knit side of these thinly stranded pieces curl to the inside to make the purl side the exposed outside.

This project was knit with:

Sassy Skein's Key West Karibbean Kotton, Aran weight, 100% mercerized cotton, 1.75oz/50g = approx 74yd/67m per ball
(A) 3 balls, color #224
(B) 3 balls, color #222
(C) 3 balls, color #216

Strings and Stripes Socks

So snazzy, I don't want to wear

SKILL LEVEL

Intermediate

SIZES

Small (Large)

FINISHED MEASUREMENTS

Cuff to heel 7 (8½)"/18 (22)cm
Heel to toe 7 (8½)"/18 (22)cm

MATERIALS AND TOOLS

Approx total: 315yd/284m of DK
  weight yarn, cotton
Color A: 105yd/95m of 3 DK weight
  yarn, cotton, in ecru
Color B: 105yd/95m of 3 DK weight
  yarn, cotton, in dark blue
Color C: 105yd/95m of 3 DK weight
  yarn, cotton, in red
Knitting needles: 3.75mm (size 5 U.S.)
  straight and set of 4 double-pointed *or
  size to obtain gauge*
Stitch marker
Stitch holder
Tapestry needle

shoes over them.

GAUGE

26 sts and 32 rows = 4"/10cm in
Stockinette Stitch (knit on RS, purl
on WS)
Always take time to check your gauge.

SPECIAL ABBREVIATION

Slip, slip, knit (ssk): slip 1 knitwise, slip
1 knitwise, K2 slipped stitches together
through back loop - 1 decrease has
been made

PATTERN STITCH

K1, P1 RIBBING

Round 1: *K1, p1; repeat from * around.

Repeat round 1 for pattern.

Sock (make 2)

TOP RUFFLE

With C, cast on 80 (88) sts.

Row 1 (WS): Purl.

Row 2 (RS): Knit.

Row 3: P2tog across—40 (44) sts.

Work K1, P1 Rib for 5 rows.

Next row (WS): Knit.

LEG

With RS facing, distribute sts on three
double-pointed needles, as follows:

Note: The beginning of the round or
row for this sock pattern is worked from
the center back between needle #2 and
needle #3.

Round 1: With A, k14 (15) onto needle #3,
k12 (14) sts onto needle #1 for instep and
k14 (15) sts on needle #2. Join to work
sts in the round; place marker between
needles #2 and #3 to indicate beginning
of round.

Round 2: With A, knit.

Rounds 3 and 4: With B, knit.

Rounds 5–36 (44): Knit 30 (38) more
rounds in the following color sequence:
*2 rows with A, 2 rows with B. For small
size only, decrease 1 st each on needles
#3 and #2 when working last rnd—38
(44) sts.

Redistribute sts as follows:

Rnd 37 (45): With B, k13 (15) on needle
#3 and slip last 4 of these sts onto needle
#1, k12 (14) sts on needle #1; k4 sts
on needle #2 and slip these 4 sts onto
needle #1; knit remaining 9 (11) sts on
needle #2.

Row 38 (46): Knit across sts on needles #2 and #3 and combine these sts onto one needle. These 18 (22) sts are worked back and forth in rows to form heel flap.

Knit across 20 (22) sts on needle #1 and place on a stitch holder for instep to be worked later.

HEEL FLAP

Row 1: With WS of heel facing, attach B, sl 1, purl all remaining sts.

Row 2 (RS): With B, *sl 1, k1; repeat from * to end.

Row 3 (WS): With B, sl 1, purl remaining sts.

Rows 4–17 (19): Repeat last 2 rows in the following color sequence: *2 rows with C, 2 rows with B; repeat from * to end.

TURN HEEL

Work following rows with C.

Row 1 (WS): P9 (12), p2tog, p1, turn.

Row 2: Sl 1, k3 (5), ssk, k1, turn.

Row 3: Sl 1, p4 (6), p2tog, p1, turn.

Row 4: Sl 1, k5 (7), ssk, k1, turn.

Row 5: Sl 1, p6 (8), p2tog, p1, turn.

Row 6: Sl 1, k7 (9), ssk, k1, turn.

Row 7: Sl 1, p8 (10), p2tog, p1, turn—11 (13) sts.

Larger size only:

Row 8: Sl 1, k11, ssk, turn.

Row 9: Sl 1, p11, p2tog—13 sts.

INSTEP

Redistribute stitches as follows: With RS of heel facing and B, knit the first 6 (7) sts of the heel onto a spare needle and hold away from work. Continuing on the heel sts for needle #3, knit the remaining 5 (6) sts and pick up and knit 12 (13) sts along left side of heel flap—17 (19) sts on needle #3. For needle # 1, work across the instep sts—20 (22) sts on needle #1. For needle #2, pick up and knit 11 (12) sts along right side of heel flap, then knit 6 (7) heel sts on spare needle—17 (19) sts on needle #2.

Round 1: Join A in middle of heel between needles #2 and #3, knit.

Round 2:

Needle #3: Knit to last 3 sts, ssk, k1;

Needle #1: Knit;

Needle #2: K1, k2tog, knit to end.

Repeat rounds 1 and 2 in following color sequence: 3 more rows with A, *5 rows with B, 5 rows with A; repeat from * until needles #2 and #3 each have 10 (11) sts remaining.

Work rounds in established pattern, without further decreasing, until the foot, measured from the heel, measures 5½ (7)"/14 (18)cm. End after completing 5 rows of last color and ready to work sts from needle #1.

SHAPE TOE

Change to C.

Round 1:

Needle #1: K1, k2tog, knit to last 3 sts, ssk, k1;

Needle #2: K1, k2tog, knit to end;

Needle #3: Knit to last 3 sts, ssk, k1.

Round 2: Knit.

Repeat last 2 rounds until 8 sts remain on needle #1, and 4 sts remain on needles #2 and #3. Slip sts from needle #3 onto needle #2, so there are two needles with 8 sts on each. Cut yarn, leaving a 30"/76cm tail to weave toe sts together.

FINISHING

Sew small opening at back of top ruffle. Tie off and weave in all ends (except long tail for finishing toe).

KITCHENER STITCH TO FINISH TOE

Thread long tail onto tapestry needle.

Step 1: With WS together, hold both knitting needles together and even, and insert tapestry needle into first st on front needle as if to purl. Draw yarn through. Leave st on needle.

Step 2: Hold yarn in back, insert tapestry needle as if to knit into first st on back needle, and draw yarn through. Leave st on needle.

Step 3: Hold yarn in front, insert tapestry needle as if to knit through first st on front needle, and draw yarn through. Slip st off needle. Insert tapestry needle through next st on front needle as if to purl, and draw yarn through. Leave st on needle.

Step 4: Insert tapestry needle as if to purl through first st on back needle, and draw yarn through. Slip st off needle. Insert tapestry needle through next st on back needle as if to knit, and draw yarn through. Leave st on needle.

Repeat steps 3 and 4 until all but 1 st have been eliminated. Draw yarn through this st to secure.

POM-POM (MAKE TWO, OPTIONAL)

With C, make two pom-poms as described on page 17. Secure one pom-pom just below top ruffle of each sock.

This project was knit with:

• • • • • • • • • • • • • • • • • •

Sassy Skein's Key West Karibbean Kotton, DK weight, 100% mercerized cotton, 1.75oz/50g = approx 105yd/95m per ball

(A) 1 ball, color #124
(B) 1 ball, color #122
(C) 1 ball, color #116

Pink Parfait Scarf

Easy

SIZES

Small (Large)

FINISHED MEASUREMENTS

Width 4½"/11cm
Length 66 (76)"/168 (193)cm, excluding
    edging

Sugar and spice,

MATERIALS AND TOOLS

Approx total: 324 (540)yd/292 (486)m of
    (**4**) worsted weight yarn, baby alpaca
Color A: 108 (216)yd/97 (194)m of (**4**)
    worsted weight yarn, baby alpaca,
    in raspberry
Color B: 108 (216)yd/97 (194)m of (**4**)
    worsted weight yarn, baby
        alpaca, in pink
    Color C: 108 (108)yd/97 (97)m
        of (**4**) worsted weight yarn,
        baby alpaca, in gray
    Knitting needles: 6mm (size 10
U.S.) *or size to obtain gauge*
    Crochet hook for Lizzie loops
    (optional)
Tapestry needle

GAUGE

16 sts and 18 rows = 4"/10cm in Wide Rib Stitch

Always take time to check your gauge.

PATTERN STITCH

WIDE RIB STITCH

Row 1 (RS): K2, p3, *k3, p3; repeat from * once, k2.

Row 2 (WS): P2, k3, *p3, k3; repeat from * once, p2.

Repeat rows 1 and 2 for pattern.

OPENWORK END

Rows 1–5 (WS): With B, knit.

Row 6: K2, *yo, k2tog; repeat from * to last st, k1.

Repeat rows 1–6 6 (8) more times.

Repeat rows 1–5.

FINISHING

Decoration on ends of scarf is optional. The scarf, as shown, has Lizzie loops, in all three colors, worked along each short edge.

Weave in ends carefully so that both sides of the scarf are clean and smooth.

Note: See page 18 for more information on making Lizzie loops.

This project was knit with:

Blue Sky Alpaca's Baby Alpaca, worsted weight, 100% baby alpaca, 3.5oz/100g = approx 108yd/97m per ball

(A) 1 (2) balls, color #551

(B) 1 (2) balls, color #555

(C) 1 ball, color #570

and everything nice...

Scarf

OPENWORK END

With A, cast on 19 sts.

Rows 1–5 (WS): Knit (Garter St).

Row 6: K2, *yo, k2tog; repeat from * to last st, k1.

Repeat 1st 6 rows 6 (8) more times.

Repeat rows 1–5.

RIB SECTION

Work Wide Rib Stitch for 22 (25)"/56 (64)cm.

Change to B, work Wide Rib Stitch for 22 (25)"/56 (64)cm. End with a RS row.

Pink Parfait Hat

SKILL LEVEL

Easy

SIZES

Small (Large)

FINISHED MEASUREMENTS

Circumference 16 (18½)"/41 (47)cm
Height 8 (9½)"/20 (24)cm

MATERIALS AND TOOLS

Approx total: 324yd/292m of (4) worsted
    weight yarn, baby alpaca
Color A: 108yd/97m of (4) worsted
    weight yarn, baby alpaca,
    in raspberry
Color B: 108yd/97m of (4) worsted
    weight yarn, baby alpaca, in pink
Color C: 108yd/97m of (4) worsted
    weight yarn, baby alpaca, in gray
Knitting needles: 5mm (size 8 U.S.) *or size
    to obtain gauge*
Tapestry needle

GAUGE

17 sts and 26 rows = 4"/10cm in K3, P3 Rib
Always take time to check your gauge.

PATTERN STITCH

K3, P3 RIB

Row 1: *K3, p3; repeat from * to end.
Repeat row 1 for pattern.

I'm tickled pink, from my head to my toes.

Hat

Note: This piece is not knit in the round.

HAT BAND

With A, cast on 71 (77) sts.

Rows 1–5 (WS): Knit (Garter St).

Row 6: With C, k2, *yo, k2tog; repeat from * to last st, k1.

Rows 7–11: With C, knit.

Row 12: With B, k2, *yo, k2tog; repeat from * to last st, k1.

Rows 13–17: With B, knit.

BODY

Next row (RS): *K3, p3; repeat from * to end, increasing 1 st—72 (78) sts.

Work K3, P3 Rib until hat measures 6 (7½)"/15 (19)cm. End with a WS row.

With A, work 4 (6) rows in K3, P3 Rib.

Next row (RS): Purl.

Next row: *K1, k2tog, p3; repeat from * to end—60 (65) sts.

Next row (RS): *K3, p2; repeat from * to end.

Next row (WS): *K2, p3; repeat from * to end.

Repeat last 2 rows 4 more times.

Bind off loosely, leaving a long yarn tail.

FINISHING

With yarn tail, sew back seam. Weave in ends on wrong side of hat. Hold one strand of each color together. Use a crochet hook to weave the strands in and out of the ribbing just above the "all purl" row. Pull the strands tightly to gather the top. Tie off the strands of yarn as you choose. As shown, they are tied in a decorative bow.

This project was knit with:

Blue Sky Alpaca's Baby Alpaca, worsted weight, 100% baby alpaca, 3.5oz/100g = approx 108yd/97m per ball
(A) 1 ball, color #551
(B) 1 ball, color #555
(C) 1 ball, color #570

Derby Duds

Giggles make these corkscrews jiggle.

SKILL LEVEL

Easy

SIZES

Small (Large)

FINISHED MEASUREMENTS

Circumference 16 (19)"/41 (48)cm
Height 7 (9)"/18 (23)cm

MATERIALS AND TOOLS

Approx total: 400yd/360m of (4) worsted
weight yarn, acrylic/wool

COLORWAY #1:

Color A: 200yd/180m of (4) worsted
weight yarn, acrylic/wool, in lime green
Color B: 200yd/180m of (4) worsted
weight yarn, acrylic/wool, in purple

COLORWAY #2:

Reverse colors A and B
Knitting needles: 3.75mm (size 5 U.S.)
10–12"/25–31cm circular needle and
set of 4 double-pointed needles or size
to obtain gauge
Stitch markers
Tapestry needle

GAUGE

20 sts and 28 rows = 4"/10cm in
Stockinette Stitch (knit every round)
Always take time to check your gauge.

SPECIAL ABBREVIATIONS

**Knit into front and back of stitch
(kf&b):** Insert needle into front of
st to knit the stitch as usual, but do
not remove st from needle. Knit into
the back of same st, and remove st
from needle.

Hat

With A and circular needle, cast on 120
(138) sts. Lay sts down on a flat surface
to be sure that the cast-on sts are not
twisted. Place a marker to indicate the
beginning of the round. Join to work sts in
the round.

Round 1: Knit.

Round 2: Purl.

Rounds 3–6 (7): Knit.

Round 7 (8): *K1, k2tog; repeat from *
around—80 (92) sts.

Round 8 (9): K39 (45), k2tog, knit
around—79 (91) sts.

HAT BAND

Rounds 1–9 (10): With B, *k1, p1; repeat
from * around.

With A, knit all sts in rounds until hat
measures 4 (6)"/10 (15)cm from bottom of
hat band.

Next round: K39 (45), k2tog, knit
around—78 (90) sts.

CROWN

Redistribute stitches on 3 double-pointed
needles and continue to work in the
round with RS facing.

Round 1: *K11 (13), k2tog, place marker;
repeat from * 5 more times—72 (84) sts.

Round 2: *Knit to within 2 sts of marker,
k2tog; repeat from * 5 more times, knit
around—66 (78) sts.

Repeat round 2 until 6 sts remain. Cut
yarn, leaving a long tail. Thread tail
through remaining 6 sts, pull tight, and
tie off.

FINISHING

Weave in yarn tails on WS of hat.

The hat can be trimmed with any
combination of corkscrews and I-cord.
Use individual creativity as to yarn color
and placement.

CORKSCREW

In color of choice, cast on 12 (16) sts. Work back and forth in rows.

Row 1: Kf&b in each st—24 (32) sts.

Bind off very loosely, leaving a long tail to secure corkscrew to top of hat.

I-CORD

With 2 strands of yarn held together, make one I-cord 3"/8cm long.

Coil I-cord and sew to top of hat. Sew corkscrews to top of hat. Weave in all ends.

Note: See page 104 for more information on making I-cord.

This project was knit with:
. . . .

Plymouth Yarn's Encore, worsted weight, 75% acrylic/25% washable wool, 3.5oz/ 100g = approx 200yd/180m per ball
(A) 1 ball, color #3335
(B) 1 ball, color #1606

Bella Bolero

Get ready to cha-cha.

SKILL LEVEL

Intermediate

SIZES

Small (Medium, Large)

FINISHED MEASUREMENTS

Chest 28 (32, 34)"/71 (81, 86)cm
Length 10½ (12, 13½)"/27 (31, 34)cm,
    including ruffle

MATERIALS AND TOOLS

Approx total: 545 (654, 763)yd/490
    (589, 687)m of (3) DK weight yarn,
    superwash wool
Color A: 436 (545, 654)yd/392 (490, 589)m
    of (3) DK weight yarn, superwash
    wool/bamboo, in red
Color B: 109 (109, 109)m/98 (98, 98)m of
    (3) DK weight yarn, superwash wool/
    bamboo, in orange
Knitting needle: 5mm (size 8 U.S.) 24–
    36"/61–91cm circular needle or size to
    obtain gauge
5mm (size 8 U.S.) set of 2 double-pointed
    needles for I-cord
Stitch holders
Tapestry needle
Crochet hook

GAUGE

22 sts and 28 rows = 4"/10cm in Staggered
    Eyelet Stitch
Always take time to check your gauge.

SPECIAL ABBREVIATIONS

Make one stitch (M1): Pick up the
    horizontal strand lying between the
    stitch just worked and the next stitch;
    knit the newly picked-up stitch through
    the back loop (increase made).
Slip, knit, pass slip stitch over (skp):
    Sl1, k1, pass slip st over knit st
    (decrease made).

STAGGERED EYELET STITCH

Row 1 (RS): Knit.

Row 2 (WS): Purl.

Row 3: *K2, k2tog, yo; repeat from *, end k3.

Row 4: Purl.

Row 5: Knit.

Row 6: Purl.

Row 7: *K2tog, yo, k2; repeat from *, end k2tog, yo, k1.

Row 8: Purl.

Repeat rows 1–8 for pattern.

Notes:

1) The Staggered Eyelet portion of this garment is worked as one piece starting with the back, increasing on both edges for the sleeves, over the shoulders, and continuing down the front to the channel for the I-cord tie. This garment does not have shoulder seams.

2) Work all rows in the eight-row Staggered Eyelet Stitch pattern until instructed to discontinue.

3) All parts of the bolero, except the edging, are worked back and forth on a circular needle. The edging is worked in rounds on the circular needle.

Bolero
BODY

Beginning at lower back edge, with A cast on 75 (87, 99) sts.

Beginning with row 2 of Staggered Eyelet Stitch, work in pattern for a total of 28 (32, 36) rows.

SHAPE SLEEVES

Increase row (RS): Cast on 18 (22, 26) sts; continue in Staggered Eyelet Stitch to end; cast on 18 (22, 26) sts at end of row—111 (131, 151) sts.

Next row: Purl.

Repeat increase row—147 (175, 203) sts.

Note: The 147 (175, 203) sts consist of 36 (44, 52) sts for each sleeve and 75 (87, 99) sts for the body.

Continue in Staggered Eyelet Stitch until piece measures 9½ (11, 12½)"/24 (28, 32)cm from beginning, ending with a WS row.

SHAPE NECK (DIVIDE FOR FRONTS)

Next row (RS): Work in Staggered Eyelet Stitch over 60 (72, 84) sts for sleeve and right front; bind off 27 (31, 35) sts for neck; continue in Staggered Eyelet Stitch to end for left front and sleeve.

Place right front and sleeve sts on st holder. Take note of which pattern row has been interrupted when the right front and sleeve sts are placed on the st holder.

LEFT FRONT AND SLEEVE

Next row (WS): Purl.

Continue in Staggered Eyelet Stitch for 8 rows.

Increase row (RS): K3, M1, continue in Staggered Eyelet Stitch to end—61 (73, 85) sts.

Continue in Staggered Eyelet Stitch for 3 rows.

Repeat last 4 rows 5 (7, 9) more times—66 (80, 94) sts.

Work even in Staggered Eyelet Stitch until left front measures the same as back to sleeve shaping when piece is folded with back neck opening even with sleeve fold. End with a RS row.

Next row (WS): Bind off 18 (22, 26) sleeve sts, purl to end—48 (58, 68) sts.

Next row: Work in Staggered Eyelet Stitch across.

Next row: Bind off 18 (22, 26) sleeve sts, purl to end—30 (36, 42) sts.

Continue in Staggered Eyelet Stitch for 3 rows.

Note: Discontinue Staggered Eyelet Stitch.

CHANNEL FOR I-CORD TIE

Work in Garter Stitch (knit every row) for 3 rows.

I-cord channel row (RS): K2, *k2tog, yo, k4; repeat from *, end k2tog, yo, k2.

Work in Garter Stitch for 3 more rows.

SHAPE LEFT LOWER EDGE

Note: Remainder of front is worked in Stockinette Stitch (knit on RS, purl on WS).

Next row (RS): Knit to last 3 sts, k2tog, k1—29 (35, 41) sts.

Next row: Purl.

Repeat the last 2 rows 4 (5, 7) more times—25 (30, 34) sts.

Next row: Knit.

Next row: Bind off 2 sts, purl to end—23 (28, 32) sts.

Next row: Knit.

Next row: Bind off 3 sts, purl to end—20 (25, 29) sts.

Next row: Knit.

Next row: Bind off 4 sts, purl to end—16 (21, 25) sts.

Next row: Knit.

Next row: Bind off 5 sts, purl to end—11 (16, 20) sts.

Next row: Knit.

Next row: Bind off 6 sts, purl to end—5 (10, 14) sts.

Next row: Knit.

Work even in Stockinette Stitch until front measures 9½ (12, 13½)"/24 (31, 34)cm from top fold. Bind off.

RIGHT FRONT

Pick up sts from st holder, rejoin yarn at neck edge, and resume Staggered Eyelet Stitch on row at which right front sts were placed on holder. Continue in Staggered Eyelet Stitch as for left front through the I-cord channel, reversing M1 shaping for right front edge and sleeve bind off.

SHAPE RIGHT LOWER EDGE

Next row (RS): K1, skp, knit to end—29 (35, 41) sts.

Next row (WS): Purl.

Repeat the last 2 rows 4 (5, 7) more times—25 (30, 34) sts.

Next row (RS): Bind off 2 sts, knit to end—23 (28, 32) sts.

Next row: Purl.

Next row: Bind off 3 sts, knit to end—20 (25, 29) sts.

Next row: Purl.

Next row: Bind off 4 sts, knit to end—16 (21, 25) sts.

Next row: Purl.

Next row: Bind off 5 sts, knit to end—11 (16, 20) sts.

Next row: Purl.

Next row: Bind off 6 sts, knit to end—5 (10, 14) sts.

Next row: Purl.

Work even in Stockinette Stitch until front measures 9½ (12, 13½)"/24 (31, 34)cm from top fold. Bind off.

FINISHING

SLEEVE EDGING

With right side facing and B, pick up 36 (40, 44) sts along sleeve edge. Work in Reverse Stockinette Stitch (purl on RS, knit on WS) for 4 (5, 6) rows.

Next row (WS): Join A (from WS) and bind off with A.

Sew sleeve and side seams.

EDGING

With right side facing and B, beginning beneath I-cord channel of right front, pick up and purl 200 (224, 248) sts around entire edge of garment. When you return to where you started, right side still facing, purl all sts for two more rounds. Do not cut B, as it will be used for the ruffle.

Beginning beneath I-cord channel of left front, with wrong side facing, join A, bind off sts working up left front, across neck and down right front to beneath I-cord channel of right front. Cut A.

. . . .

Design Tip

Always work on a flat surface when weaving side and sleeve seams. Neatly finished seams are critical to a professional-looking garment.

. . . .

RUFFLE

Note: The ruffle is worked only on the lower portion of the garment, from beneath one I-cord channel, working down right front, along lower edge, and up left front to beneath opposite I-cord channel.

With WS facing, pick up B (where it is still attached), purl sts down right front, along lower edge, and up left front, ending beneath left I-cord channel.

Next row (RS): Knit, increasing 1 st in every other st.

Next row (WS): Purl, increasing 1 st in every st. Cut B.

Next row (RS): Join A, knit.

Next row (WS): Bind off as if to knit.

TIES

With A and two double-pointed needles, cast on 3 sts. Make two I-cords, 18–20"/46–51cm long.

Weave ties through I-cord channels and secure on wrong side of sides. Cut 12 strands of B, 3"/8cm long. Hold six strands together and fold in half, forming a loop. With crochet hook, draw loop through end of one tie, draw ends through loop, and pull tight. Repeat with other six strands on end of other tie.

Weave in ends on wrong side of garment. Steam very lightly, and do not put iron or steam equipment directly on garment.

Note: See page 104 for information on making I-cord.

This project was knit with:
. . . .

Skacel's Austermann Bambou Soft, DK weight, 65% merino superwash wool/35% bamboo, 1.75oz/50g = approx 109yd/98m per ball
(A) 4 (5, 6) balls, color #011
(B) 1 ball, color #009

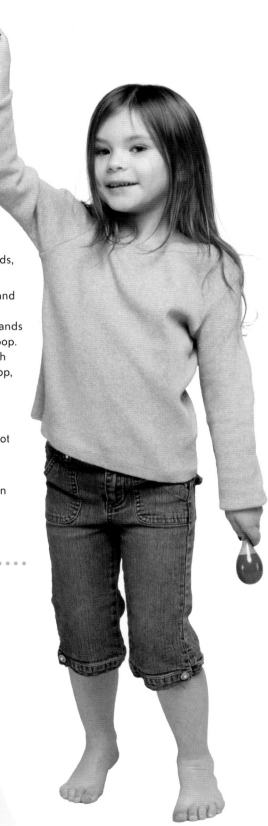

Button Bag

Cute as a button and

SKILL LEVEL

Easy

FINISHED MEASUREMENTS

Approx 8½"/22cm wide x 9½"/24cm tall,
   excluding handle
Handle 26"/66cm

MATERIALS AND TOOLS

Approx total: 370yd/333m of ❹ Aran
   weight yarn, cotton
Color A: 148yd/133m of ❹ Aran weight
   yarn, cotton, in pink
Color B: 222yd/200m of ❹ Aran weight
   yarn, cotton, in green
Knitting needles: 5mm (size 8 U.S.) *or size
   to obtain gauge*
Tapestry needle (with a small eye) for
   sewing seams and buttons
1 orange button, ⅝"/16mm
1 yellow button, ⅞"/22mm

GAUGE

16 sts and 20 rows = 4"/10cm in Wide
   Rib Stitch with two strands of yarn
   held together
Always take time to check your gauge.

PATTERN STITCH

WIDE RIB STITCH

Row 1 (RS): *K5, p1; repeat from * to last
5 sts, k5.

Row 2 (WS): Purl.

Repeat rows 1 and 2 for pattern.

Bag

With two strands of A held together, cast on 35 sts.

Work 10 rows in Garter Stitch (knit every row).

Next row (WS): Change to two strands of B held together, purl.

Work in Wide Rib Stitch until piece measures 18"/46cm. End with a WS row.

Change to two strands of A held together, work 10 rows in Garter Stitch. Bind off.

FINISHING

Fold bag in half with right sides together and bring A edges together at top of bag. Sew side seams together. Turn bag right side out.

totes your stuff, too.

HANDLE

With two strands of A held together, pick up and knit 7 sts centered across top of one side seam. Work in Garter Stitch until handle measures 26"/66cm. Bind off, leaving a long tail for sewing. With tail, sew end of handle overlapping A edge at top of bag and with side edge of handle aligning with opposite side seam.

BUTTON DETAIL

Stack small button on top of large button. Center buttons over last 2"/5cm of handle, and sew in place with a French Knot.

Weave in ends on wrong side of bag. Lightly block bag, if desired.

Note: This project is worked double stranded. Hold two strands of yarn together throughout.

Note: See page 108 for information on French Knots.

This project was knit with:

• •

Sassy Skein's Key West Karibbean Kotton, Aran weight, 100% mercerized cotton, 1.75oz/50g = approx 74yd/68m per ball
(A) 2 balls, color #206
(B) 3 balls, color #204

Little Black Bag

This bag's stylin', just like me.

SKILL LEVEL

Beginner

FINISHED MEASUREMENTS

Bag 6 x 9"/15 x 23cm
Handle 26"/66cm

MATERIALS AND TOOLS

Approx total: 296yd/266m of (4) Aran weight yarn, cotton
Color A: 222yd/200m of (4) Aran weight yarn, cotton, in black
Color B: 74yd/67m of (4) Aran weight yarn, cotton, in white
Knitting needle: 5mm (size 8 U.S.) *or size to obtain gauge*
Tapestry needle
1 black and white button, 1½"/38mm
1 yd/.9m black and white checkered ribbon, ½"/1cm wide

GAUGE

16 sts and 20 rows = 4"/10cm in Garter Stitch (knit every row) with two strands of yarn held together
Always take time to check your gauge.

Bag

With two strands of A held together, cast on 35 sts.

Work in Garter Stitch until piece measures 13"/33cm.

Bind off.

FINISHING

Fold bag in half, bringing cast-on edge up to meet bind-off edge. With A and yarn needle, sew cast-on edge to bind-off edge, and sew lower edges together. Weave in ends on wrong side of bag.

Turn bag right side out. Lightly block bag if desired.

With A, sew button to front of bag about 2½"/6cm from top edge. Weave ribbon through top edge of bag and tie in a bow.

STRAP

Cut eight 6yd/5.5m lengths of each color. Make a strap by following the Braided Strap instructions on page 19.

Repeat the steps until the handle is 24"/61cm long or desired length. Tie off your work and cut the excess strands to the same length as the first end. Sew the handle to bag.

Note: The handle can also be created by making an I-cord, or by crocheting three chains and then braiding the chains together.

This project was knit with:

Sassy Skein's Key West Karibbean Kotton, Aran weight, 100% mercerized cotton, 1.75oz/50g = approx 74yd/67m per ball

(A) 3 balls, color #201
(B) 1 ball, color #202

Vested

SKILL LEVEL

Intermediate

SIZES

4 (6, 8)

FINISHED MEASUREMENTS

Chest 24 (26½, 30)"/61 (67, 76)cm
Length 12½ (13½, 14½)"/32 (34, 37)cm
Armhole 6 (7, 8)"/15 (18, 20)cm

MATERIALS AND TOOLS

Approx total: 980yd/882m of (4) worsted
   weight yarn, wool
Color A: 245yd/221m of (4) worsted
   weight yarn, wool, in black
Color B: 245yd/221m of (4) worsted
   weight yarn, wool, in teal
Color C: 245yd/221m of (4) worsted
   weight yarn, wool, in royal blue
Color D: 245yd/221m of (4) worsted
   weight yarn, wool, in orange
Knitting needles: 4.5mm (size 7 U.S.) or
   size to obtain gauge
4 stitch holders (optional)
Tapestry needle
Stitch markers
Crochet hook
5 black and white square buttons,
   ⅝–¾"/16–19mm

GAUGE

20 sts and 28 rows = 4"/10cm in
   Stockinette Stitch (knit on RS, purl
   on WS)
Always take time to check your gauge.

SPECIAL ABBREVIATIONS

**Knit into front and back of stitch
(kf&b):** Insert needle into front of
st to knit the stitch as usual, but do
not remove st from needle. Knit into
the back of same st and remove st
from needle.

Stand up and take a bow—or two or three.

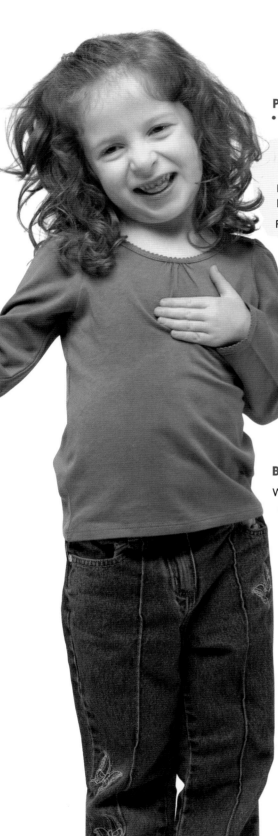

PATTERN STITCHES

. . . .

BACK RIB STITCH

Row 1 (WS): Purl.

Row 2 (RS): P1, *k3, p1; repeat from * to last st, p1.

Repeat rows 1 and 2 for pattern.

RIGHT FRONT STRIPE STITCH

Row 1 (RS): Knit.

Row 2 (WS): Purl.

Rows 3 and 4: Repeat rows 1 and 2.

Row 5 (RS): With A, *k1, p1; repeat from *.

Row 6: Purl.

Repeat rows 1–6 for pattern.

Vest

BACK

With A, cast on 58 (66, 74) sts.

Work Back Rib Stitch until back measures 6½"/17cm (all sizes) from beginning.

SHAPE ARMHOLES

Bind off 8 (9, 10) sts at beginning of next 2 rows—42 (48, 54) sts.

Decrease 1 st at beginning of next 4 rows—38 (44, 50) sts.

Work in Rib Stitch until back measures 12½ (13½, 14½)"/32 (34, 37)cm from beginning.

Next row: Bind off first 10 (11, 12) sts for shoulder (as an alternative to binding off shoulder stitches, you can place the stitches on stitch holders and use the 3-needle bind-off technique to join the shoulder seams); bind off center 18 (22, 26) sts for neck; bind off remaining 10 (11, 12) sts for other shoulder (or place on stitch holder).

LEFT SOLID COLOR FRONT

With B, cast on 4 sts.

Work in Stockinette Stitch (knit on RS, purl on WS), increase 1 st each edge (kf&b) every row until there are 30 (34, 38) sts.

Continue even in Stockinette Stitch until front measures 6½"/17cm (all sizes) from beginning, measured along straight side seam edge. End with a WS row.

SHAPE ARMHOLE

Row 1 (RS): Bind off 8 (9, 10) sts, knit to end—22 (25, 28) sts.

Row 2: Purl.

Row 3: K2tog, knit to end—21 (24, 27) sts.

RIGHT STRIPED FRONT

With C, cast on 4 sts.

Work in Right Front Stripe Stitch, increase 1 st each edge every row, in following color sequence: *4 rows with C, 2 rows with A, 4 rows with B, 2 rows with A, 4 rows with D, 2 rows with A; repeat from * until there are 30 (34, 38) sts.

Continue even in Right Front Stripe Stitch until front measures 6½"/17cm (all sizes) from beginning, measured along straight side seam edge.

SHAPE ARMHOLE AND V-NECK

Complete as for left front, reversing armhole and neck shaping, continuing in Right Front Stripe Stitch.

FINISHING

Sew side seams. Sew shoulder seams (or join them with 3-needle bind-off method).

SHAPE V-NECK

Row 1 (WS): Bind off 1 st, purl to end—19 (22, 25) sts.

Row 2 (RS): Knit.

Repeat rows 1 and 2 until there are 10 (11, 12) sts remaining.

Work even in Stockinette Stitch until front measures 12½ (13½, 14½)"/32 (34, 37)cm. Bind off shoulder sts (or place them on a stitch holder).

Repeat rows 2 and 3—20 (23, 26) sts.

Work even in Stockinette Stitch until front measures 9 (9½, 10)"/23 (24, 25)cm from beginning. End with a RS row.

Design Tip

Always work on a flat surface when weaving side and sleeve seams. Neatly finished seams are critical to a professional-looking garment.

Place markers evenly spaced along one front (right front for girl, left front for boy) to indicate buttonhole placement. With right side facing, join A in shoulder seam, single crochet around edges of vest, chain 4 when each buttonhole marker is reached (buttonhole made). Join with slip st in first single crochet and fasten off.

Weave in ends on wrong side of vest. Lightly block vest.

Sew buttons opposite buttonholes.

Note: See page 105 for information about 3-needle bind off.

Design Tip

Be creative with color. You can change color from what you see. You don't have to make the "purple sweater purple." And, boys don't have to wear brown. Ask kids what color they want to wear.

This project was knit with:

Brown Sheep's Nature Spun, worsted weight, 100% wool, 3.5oz/100g = approx 245yd/221m per ball

(A) 1 ball, color #601
(B) 1 ball, color #N78
(C) 1 ball, color #116
(D) 1 ball, color #N54

Beautiful Belt

SKILL LEVEL

Easy

SIZES

Small (Medium, Large)

FINISHED MEASUREMENTS

Approx 48 (50, 52) x 2"/122 (127, 132) x 5cm, excluding fringe

MATERIALS AND TOOLS

122yd/110m of (5) chunky weight yarn, polyester suede, in scarlet
Knitting needles: 6mm (size 10 U.S.) or size to obtain gauge
Sewing needle for sewing jewels and beads
Scarlet sewing thread
Star jewels
Crystal clear glass beads, 4mm
Crochet hook

GAUGE

16 sts and 20 rows = 4"/10cm in Seed Stitch
Always take time to check your gauge.

PATTERN STITCH

SEED STITCH (on odd number of stitches)

Row 1 (RS): *K1, p1; repeat from *, end k1.

Repeat row 1 for pattern.

This belt isn't shy~

Belt

With A, cast on 7 sts.

Work in Seed Stitch until belt measures 48 (50, 52)"/122 (127, 132)cm from beginning. Bind off in pattern.

FINISHING

Gently pull belt to smooth it. Do not block polyester yarn with an iron. Lay the belt flat and begin embellishment work. Starting at one end of the belt, using the sewing needle and scarlet sewing thread, sew each jewel in place using a bead to secure the center. Run your thread from one jewel to the next along the wrong side of your belt, hiding the thread so it does not show on either side. After all of your jewels are sewn on, add more crystal beads. Again using thread and needle, sew each bead in place, carefully running the thread along the wrong side of the belt so it does not show on either side.

and neither am I.

FRINGE

Make three tassels on each end. Cut 11 (11, 13)"/28 (28, 33)cm lengths of yarn. Fold three strands of yarn in half for each tassel, forming a loop. Using a crochet hook, draw the tassel loop through a secure place at the end of the belt. Draw the ends of the fringe through the loop and pull tightly. Include the tail of yarn from your cast on and bind off in with the appropriate tassels. After all of your tassels are in place, trim the ends of your fringe evenly to desired length.

Note: See page 17 for more information on making fringe.

This project was knit with:

Lion Brand's Lion Suede, 100% polyester, chunky weight, 3oz/85g = approx 122yd/110m per ball, 1 ball color #113

Knitting Techniques and Patterns

There are a variety of popular stitches that become the mainstay of every knitter's repertoire. Most knitted projects are defined by the type of stitch work used to create them, and we have used many of these stitches throughout this book. What follows is a brief explanation of basic stitches and techniques.

It suffices to say that we all have our favorite method for each. If you're a new knitter, find a method that gives you the finished look that appeals to you. In most cases, it's a good idea to follow the stitch directions for the pattern you have chosen. However, if you're an experienced knitter, you may want to spread your wings and work a project in your own favorite stitch.

Techniques

CASTING ON

Single Cast On

The Single Cast On may be the easiest method to put stitches on your needle.

1. Leaving a short tail of yarn, place a slip knot on the needle in your right hand.

2. On your left hand, wrap the working yarn from the ball around your left thumb from front to back. Use your remaining fingers to grip the yarn firmly in your palm (figure 1).

3. With the right needle, cross over and in front of the yarn in your palm, and insert the needle up and through the loop on your thumb (figure 2).

4. Slip this loop from your thumb onto the needle, and pull the yarn from the ball to secure the stitch. You now have a slip knot and one stitch on your right-hand needle (figure 3).

5. Repeat this cast on procedure until you've created the number of stitches needed for your project on the right-hand needle.

Figure 1

Figure 2

Figure 3

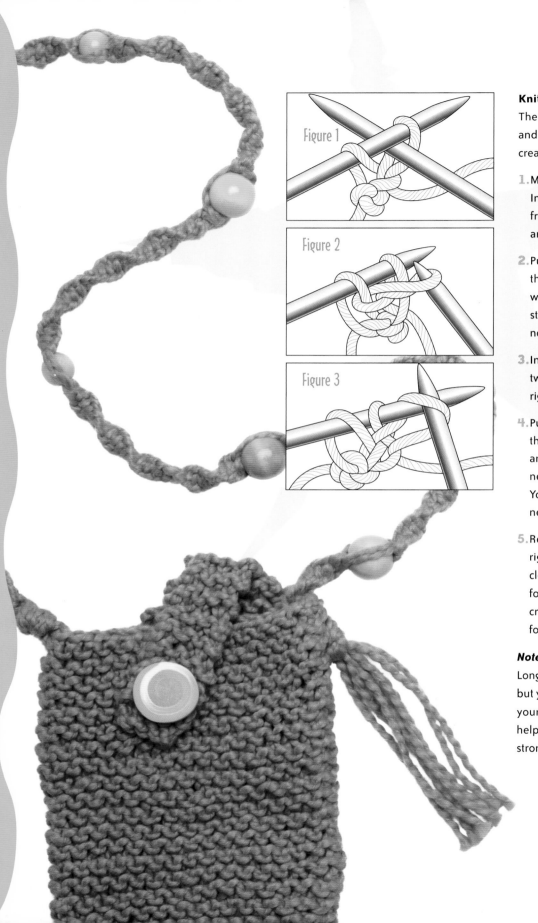

Knit On

The Knit On method uses two needles and is similar to the process you'd use to create a row of knitting.

1. Make your slip knot on the left needle. Insert the right needle into the slip knot from front to back, and wrap the yarn around the right needle as if to knit.

2. Pull the stitch on the right needle through to the front of your work, and, with a slight half turn, place the new stitch onto the left-hand needle. You now have two stitches.

3. Insert the right needle between these two stitches, and wrap yarn around the right needle as if to knit (figure 1).

4. Pull the stitch on the right needle through to the front of your work, and, with a slight half turn, place the new stitch onto the left-hand needle. You now have one more stitch on the needle (figure 2 & 3).

5. Repeat this process, inserting the right needle between the two stitches closest to the point of the left needle, for each new stitch until you've created the number of stitches needed for your project.

Note: The Double Cast On (Slingshot or Long Tail) is also a great method to use, but you might want to have someone from your yarn shop or an experienced knitter help you with this technique. It gives a strong, even edge and is worth learning.

Figure 1

Figure 2

Figure 3

BINDING OFF

As a way to neatly finish a project or create various shaping techniques, you will need to know how to bind off stitches to create a firm, yet pliable edge. You can bind off stitches with either a knit or a purl stitch, but your pattern will have instructions on what stitch will best serve your project design. The actual bind off procedure will be the same in either case.

1. Begin your bind off by working two stitches onto the right-hand needle.

2. Take the tip of the left-hand needle and lift the first stitch over the second stitch (figure 1) and off the end of the right needle (figure 2). You now have one stitch on the right needle (figure 3).

3. Knit or purl the next stitch so you have two stitches on the right needle.

4. Repeat this process until the designated number of stitches have been bound off for the pattern.

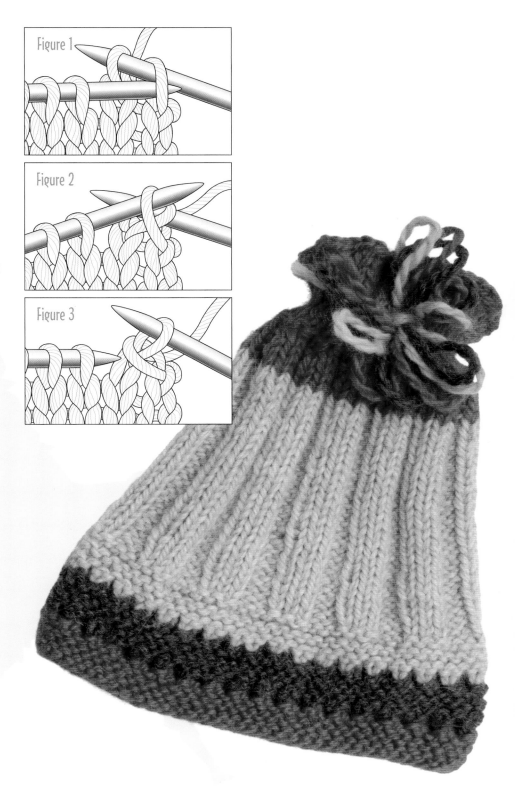

Figure 1

Figure 2

Figure 3

EASY CABLE

Cables involve a unique "crossing" of stitches and offer endless possibilities, although you should follow your specific pattern instructions. Crossing stitches requires a cable needle.

1. Following your pattern instructions as to how many and which stitches to engage, slip a specified number of stitches on your cable needle and hold these stitches either in front (wyif) or in back (wyib) of your work.

2. Work the specified number of sts from the left-hand needle to the right-hand needle.

3. Work the sts from the cable needle onto the right-hand needle.

I-CORD

I-cord is the perfect technique for creating drawstrings and edgings. As a drawstring, the cord is worked in the round and has even more substance than a flat crocheted chain. This technique works best on double-pointed needles, although you can use a circular needle.

1. Depending on the weight of the yarn and how you are using the I-Cord, cast on using the double pointed-needles, based on the pattern's guideline for the number of sts.

2. Once these sts are on the needle, do not turn your work. Instead, slide those sts to the other end of the needle, keeping the yarn in the back of the needle.

3. Pull the yarn tightly behind and across the back of the sts you have just moved and knit those sts, without turning your work.

4. Slide those sts to the end of the needle, with the yarn in back, and knit the sts again.

5. Repeat this process until you reach the desired length for the cord.

3 NEEDLE BIND OFF

1. Hold the two needles of stitches to be bound off in your left hand, with the needles pointed in the same direction. With a third needle in your right hand, insert the right-hand needle into the first stitch on the front needle and into the first stitch on the back needle, as if to knit (figure 1). Knit these two stitches at the same time.

2. Repeat this step for the second stitch (figure 2). Now you have two stitches on your right hand needle. Bind off the first stitch, bringing it over the second stitch in the usual fashion (figure 3). Continue working all the stitches on your left-hand needle as instructed above until you have one final stitch. Cut small tail of yarn and pull it through the stitch. Pull securely.

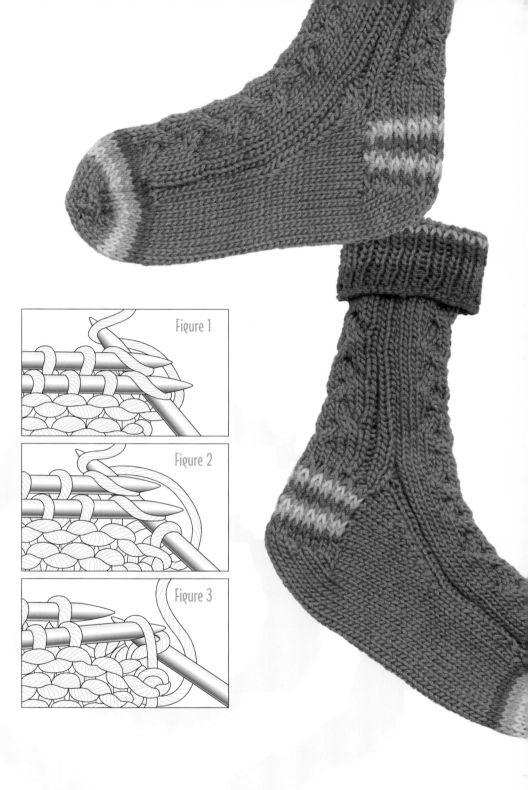

Figure 1

Figure 2

Figure 3

Figure 1

Figure 2

PICK UP STITCHES

1. With the right side of your finished piece of knitting facing you and in your left hand, take a ball of appropriate color yarn and an empty needle in your right hand. Beginning along the edge of the piece, insert your needle into the "bump" in the stitch edge, working from front to back.

2. Wrap your yarn around the needle and pull through as though you are knitting the stitch (figure 1). Work along the edge of the piece inserting your needle at each "bump," and repeat the process of wrapping the yarn and pulling through (figure 2).

Note: Your pattern will tell you how many stitches to pick up. It is important to calculate how to do this evenly. Depending on the number of stitches you need to pick up, you may have to place them closer together or farther apart than the "bumps."

Tip
Secure new yarn to the old yarn by twisting before picking up first stitch.

Pattern Stitches

STOCKINETTE STITCH

This is the most basic of all stitches and can be worked on any number of stitches.

Row 1 (RS): Knit all stitches.

Row 2 (WS): Purl all stitches.

GARTER STITCH

The Garter Stitch is quite simple and can be worked on any number of stitches.

Knit all stitches for both right and wrong side rows.

SEED STITCH

The Seed Stitch is a great way to add an attractive, bumpy texture to your knitting.

Row 1 (RS): *K1, p1, repeat from * across row.

Row 2 (WS): As the stitches face you, knit the purl sts and purl the knit stitches.

Repeat rows 1 and 2.

Tip

If you're working odd-number stitches, you will be repeating row 1 throughout.

DUPLICATE STITCH

A duplicate stitch is V-shaped, just like the Vs on your knitted piece. Envision a V with its bottom point marked as A, the top right point as B, and the top left point as C. Working from the back of your piece, bring up your needle at A, down at B, up at C, and then back down at A.

Embroidery Stitches

Embroidery stitches are a great way to further personalize your knitted creations. The two simple stitches at left are perfect for adding dimension, texture, and fun. Follow the stitch illustrations and bring your needle up at odd numbers and down at even numbers.

French Knot

Lazy Daisy Stitch

About the Authors

Mary Bonnette and Jo Lynne Murchland, owners and the creative force behind The Sassy Skein, are excited about the tremendous growth they have seen not only in their business, but in the knitting industry as a whole.

These two internationally known designers first created a name for themselves by designing hand knits for the children's market. Most recently they have been creating a splash with their line of patterns and kits for making fun and funky bags, belts, and other accessories that are not only enjoyable to knit, but are functional and a pleasure to use.

The pair have produced a "Learn to Knit" DVD that is included in all of their patterns and kits.

With an emphasis on comfort, creative styling, and the use of bright and bold color, Mary and Jo Lynne have distinguished themselves as featured designers and authors for children's knitwear.

Acknowledgments

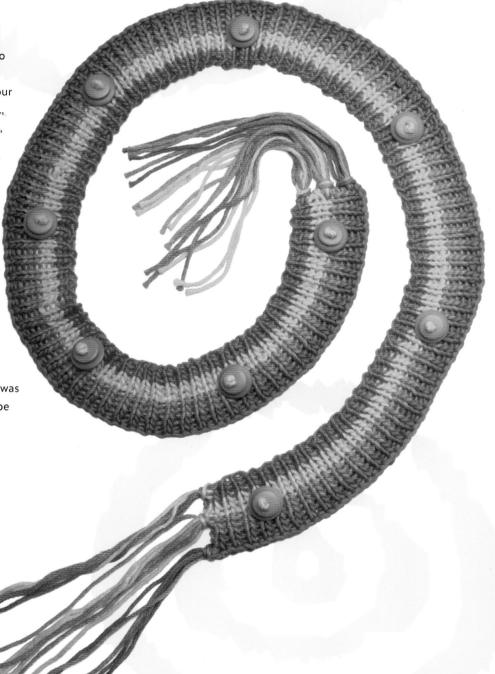

We would like to express our special thanks to the staff at Lark Books for entrusting to us their vision and enthusiasm for this book. We would also like to convey our appreciation to the following yarn companies who so generously provided their yarns for our model projects: Blue Sky Alpacas, Inc., Cascade Yarns, Skacel Collection, Inc., and The Sassy Skein, Inc. In addition, we have also included yarns from Brown Sheep, Lion Brand, and Plymouth Yarn.

Our acknowledgments would not be complete without thanking our families for their faithful support while we designed, knit, wrote, and edited patterns. For many months, our knitting bags were our constant companions, and "knit-ese" was the only language we spoke. We were not surprised, given the number of take-out meals, that it was suggested our next venture be a recipe book: *Purling with Pizza!*

Index

Abbreviations, 22

Bags, 36, 47, 58, 60, 90, 92
Beading, 20
Belt, 50, 98
Binding off, 103
Bolero, 85
Braided strap, 19
Buttons, 20

Casting On
    Knit On, 102
    Single Cast On, 101
Conversion chart, 12

Duplicate stitch, 107

Easy Cable, 104
Embroidery stitches, 21

French knot, 108
Fringe, 17

Garter stitch, 107
Gauge, 11

Hat, 27, 56, 80, 82

Intarsia, 15

Lazy daisy, 108
Leg warmers, 63
Lizzie loops, 18

Mittens, 24

Needles, 12

Pick up stitches, 106
Pillows, 52
Pom-poms, 17

Ribbing, 19
Ruffles, 18

Scarf, 44, 66, 69, 72, 78
Seed stitch, 107
Slip stitch, 16
Slippers, 33
Socks, 39, 74
Stockinette stitch, 107
Striping, 14
Supplies, 13

Three needle bind off, 105
Toy, 30

Vest, 94

Yarn
    Making substitutions, 10
    Selecting, 9

Sources and Suppliers

Usually, you can find the supplies you need for making the projects in Lark books at your local craft supply store, discount mart, home improvement center, or retail shop relevant to the topic of the book. Occasionally, however, you may need to buy materials or tools from specialty suppliers. In order to provide you with the most up-to-date information, we have created a listing of suppliers on our website, which we update on a regular basis. Visit us at www.larkbooks. com, click on "Sources," and then search for the relevant materials. You can also search by book title, vendor, and author name. Additionally, you can search for supply sources located in or near your town by entering your zip code. You will find numerous companies listed, with the web address and/or mailing address and phone number.